Procedure Writing
Principles and Practices

by

Douglas Wieringa

Christopher Moore

Valerie Barnes

Contributing Authors

Charlene R. J. Forslund

Susan G. Hill

Wendy J. Reese

Ronald Wilson

BATTELLE PRESS

Columbus • Richland

DISCLAIMER

This report was prepared as an account of work sponsored by an agency of the United States Government. Neither the United States Government nor any agency thereof, nor Battelle Memorial Institute, nor any of their employees, makes **any warranty, expressed or implied, or assumes any legal liability or responsibility for the accuracy, completeness, or usefulness of any information, apparatus, product, or process disclosed, or represents that its use would not infringe privately owned rights.** Reference herein to any specific commercial product, process, or service by trade name, trademark, manufacturer, or otherwise does not necessarily constitute or imply its endorsement, recommendation, or favoring by the United States Government or any agency thereof, or Battelle Memorial Institute. The views and opinions of authors expressed herein do not necessarily state or reflect those of the United States Government or any agency thereof.

PACIFIC NORTHWEST LABORATORY
operated by
BATTELLE MEMORIAL INSTITUTE
for the
UNITED STATES DEPARTMENT OF ENERGY
under Contract DE-AC06-76RLO 1830

Library of Congress Cataloging-in-Publication Data

Wieringa, Douglas, 1960–

  Procedure writing : principles and practices / Douglas Wieringa,
Christopher J. Moore, Valerie E. Barnes.
     p.   cm.
  Includes bibliographical references (p.   ) and index.
  ISBN 0-935470-68-9 : $34.95
   1. Technical manuals. 2. Technical writing. I. Moore,
Christopher J., 1957–   . II. Barnes, Valerie Elizabeth.
III. Title.
T11.W455 1992
808.0666—dc20

Printed in the United States of America

Battelle Press
505 King Avenue
Columbus, Ohio 43201-2693
614-424-6393
1-800-451-3543

Preface

This book was originally written for the United States Department of Energy as a guide to procedure writers in Department of Energy facilities. As we were working on it, we began to realize that, with slight modification, the principles we were presenting would be useful to procedure writers in a variety of situations.

Procedures, as we explain in Chapter 1, are instructions. Instructions are used in all sorts of situations:

- Nuclear power plants use procedures to govern most aspects of operation and maintenance.

- Procedures are used in the military, again governing the operation and maintenance of complex equipment.

- Procedures are widely used in aviation, from the cockpit checklists used by pilots to the procedures used by maintainers.

- Computer users often rely on procedures. These procedures can be part of the documentation prepared for the hardware or software or they can be written by hand as instructions from one person to another. Companies that write custom software, such as an internal accounting package, often must also write their own procedures for using that software.

- Procedures are used extensively in the petroleum industry and other hydrocarbon industries.

- The ISO 9000 Quality Standard (or most any total quality management system) requires procedures to standardize methods of doing work.

- Pharmaceutical manufacturers must have standard operating procedures in place for all phases of operations and control.

- Many other types of businesses, ranging from banks to volunteer fire departments, use procedures.

It is our hope that this book will be useful in all of these areas.

We would like to acknowledge that this book has not employed "gender-neutral" language and offer our sincere apologies to readers who may find our reliance on masculine pronouns (*he, him, himself*) offensive or insensitive. While we do strongly believe that gender-neutral language should be used whenever possible, we have found it necessary to compromise here in order to achieve a more important objective—clear communication. We have avoided using conventions such as *her or she*, *his or hers*, and *s/he* because, as the model presented in Chapter 2 suggests, these conventions impede readability and comprehension. We believe that most readers would rather not encounter such passages in this book.

This book is an attempt to meld theory and practice. Accordingly, we have drawn information from a variety of sources. Traditional books on writing, such as *The Elements of Style* (Strunk & White, 1979), *Modern American Usage* (Follett, 1966), the *Handbook of Technical Writing* (Brusaw, Alred, & Oliu, 1987), and *Words Into Type* (1974), proved valuable sources.[1] Wherever possible, we have supplemented the tried-and-proven techniques from books such as these with the results of scientific studies. Unfortunately, scientific research into procedures and into writing in general is in its infancy, and studies that present useful information for the procedure writer are not as common as we would like. Although more research is being done, the present lack of scientific research is indicative of the character of writing: "Keep in mind that, despite increasingly good research into its nature, writing is a craft and not a science" (Houp & Pearsall, 1988, p. 146).

This book represents the contributions of many individuals, all of whom played important roles. First, we must thank our project sponsors at the Department of Energy, Bob Waters and Maggie Sturdivant. Without them, this book would never have been written. Our appreciation also goes to our colleagues at EG&G Idaho, Susan Hill and Wendy Reece. Sue and Wendy contributed material to this book, edited drafts, and were always responsive to our questions. They also played an important role in our dealings with the Department of Energy. Finally, many of our colleagues at Battelle provided invaluable assistance. In no particular order, they are Charlene Forslund, who wrote and edited material; Ron Wilson, who performed the thankless task of tracking our many references and wrote some material; Sadie Johnson, who worked the long hours necessary to produce this book; Charleen Sager, whose eagle editing eye kept us all honest; and Ali Tabatabai, Bob Gruel, and David Eike, our project managers.

This book also represents all that we have learned working with procedures for over ten years. We have had the good fortune to participate in several challenging procedures-related projects during this time and must also extend our thanks to those organizations with whom we have worked. We would like to thank, in particular, the U.S. Nuclear Regulatory Commission and Arizona Public Service Corporation's Palo Verde Nuclear Generating Station. We have, in fact, drawn some of the examples in this book from Palo Verde's progressive procedures.

---

[1] In this book, references are cited by the author's name, the year of publication, and, if a quote is used, the page number.

Table of Contents

Procedure Writing
Principles and Practices

Part One:
The Basics

Chapter 1

An Introduction to Procedures

Procedures are instructions, and this book explains how to write instructions so that others can understand them. Procedures can range from simple to complex; they describe anything from booting a personal computer to operating a nuclear power plant during an emergency. Plans, mission statements, proposals, and technical articles are not procedures, although parts of these documents may be considered procedures if they present instructions. No matter how simple or complex the procedure is, certain principles govern the way it should be written. This book presents these principles.

1.1 Procedures and Why They Are Important

There are several benefits to good procedures: procedures reduce human error, document the best way to perform a task, and provide an administrative record of a procedure's execution. This section discusses these benefits. It also discusses some of the reasons that workers resist procedures and what you, the procedure writer, can do to write procedures that will be accepted.

The Benefits of Procedures

The most important function of procedures is to assist workers in the performance of tasks. Even highly skilled workers can use assistance in performing complicated tasks, particularly if a task is performed infrequently or has a high safety significance, making the consequences of an error very high. Humans are fallible; we forget things and make mistakes. Properly written procedures reduce the opportunity for these sorts of errors. By reducing error, procedures can improve quality; protect workers, the public, and machinery; and increase productivity. Chapter 2 will discuss the role procedures can play in reducing human error.

Procedures also help ensure that tasks are performed in an efficient, safe manner. A procedure represents (or should represent) a collective agreement on the best way to perform a given task. A worker following an emergency procedure, for instance, is being guided by the collective knowledge and experience of the entire procedure development team, who took the time necessary to develop and test the procedure; without a procedure, the worker must decide what to do himself, perhaps without the assistance of others and under the stress of time pressure and even physical danger. Without the procedure, he is more likely to perform the task incorrectly.

Finally, procedures serve an important administrative function. Many procedures include check-offs or sign-off blanks that are completed as the procedure is performed. Once the task is completed, the procedure can be archived as a record of the task's performance. If a problem arises later that may be connected to the performance of the procedure, investigators can retrieve the archived procedure to determine if it was executed and who signed off at quality assurance points.

Resistance to Procedures

Despite these values of procedures, workers sometimes resent procedures and resist using them, seeing them as an affront to their skills and experience and as an administrative barrier to performing tasks correctly. There are two reasons that typically lie behind this resentment, one of which you, the procedure writer, have control over.

The first factor, and the one the procedure writer is likely to have little control over, is the existence of poor working relationships between managers and workers. If workers do not get along with managers, or with each other, procedures may be seen as a scapegoat for these problems; for example, procedures may be seen as an extension or symbol of management and resented for that reason. If this is the case, those problems must be addressed before truly effective procedures can be implemented.

Fortunately, you have more control over the second reason that workers may resent procedures—the procedures do not address workers' needs. A whole host of factors can make the procedure less useful to the user. Procedures can be technically inaccurate, fail to acknowledge workers' skills, contain superficial errors that detract from the integrity of the procedure (e.g., frequent spelling errors), contain so many cross-references to other procedures that they are too difficult to use, and so on.

Procedure quality does affect the likelihood that procedures will be used; for example, in a study of maintenance procedures in commercial nuclear power plants, one of the key findings was that

> the procedures that do exist are often of such poor quality that personnel avoid or refuse to use them. In general, maintenance procedures are poorly written and difficult to follow. The inadequacy of existing procedures constitutes the single largest reason cited by maintenance

supervisors for their unwillingness to encourage procedure use.
(Morgenstern et al., 1985, p. vii)

Procedure quality is determined by the user—the worker who will be using this procedure. He is your customer. The importance of considering the user as customer became evident as we were writing this book. As part of our research, we visited various facilities that used procedures extensively and talked to procedure writers and users. The facility that seemed to have the best procedures was the facility that worked hardest to treat the users as customers. Interaction among procedure writers and procedure users was extensive; writers interviewed users before writing or revising a procedure, called users when they had questions, and had users review drafts of procedures. Without this frequent contact, the writers would not have been aware of the users' needs and would have been unable to tailor the procedures to meet those needs. It is a well-accepted principle that such audience analysis is essential to effective communication (Souther & White, 1984).

However, it is true the procedures you write may be reviewed by people who are not end-users, such as managers and auditors. You may feel more of a need to address these reviewers' comments than to address the users' comments. This could be a problem, but it should not be; if these people are reviewing your procedures properly, they will act as surrogates for the procedures' users. They should put themselves in the users' place, and suggest the changes that they believe are in the users' best interests. It is ultimately the *writer's* task to defend the interests of the users, however.

In summary, if you write procedures that address the needs of those who will be using them, there is a much greater chance that those procedures will be accepted and used. Procedures do not have to live up to their unfortunate stereotype of being impediments to accomplishing tasks.

1.2   The Importance of a Writers' Guide

This book presents general guidance on procedure preparation. If your facility only writes a few procedures, then this book will probably be sufficient guidance for you. However, if your facility develops many procedures (such as the several thousand in a nuclear power plant), then you are going to need a *writers' guide*.

A writers' guide (sometimes called a style guide) specifies the format and content of procedures at a particular facility in a very detailed manner—more detailed than this book. This book typically specifies a principle rather than a specific practice; for example, it says that the equipment cited in procedures should be identified in a consistent, unambiguous, precise manner without specifying what that manner should be. The reason for not specifying exactly how location information should be presented is that there are several ways to present location information that meet the intent of the principle. For the purposes of this book, which can be used in many different settings, it would be too restrictive to state that location information *had* to be presented in one manner.

However, the procedure writer needs to know how to present location information at his facility, because all procedures in his facility should present location information consistently. He needs guidance that reads something like this: *Identify all equipment cited in the procedure by common name and equipment number. Present the information in that order, with a comma between the name and number.* This guidance meets the criteria of the principle—it is consistent, unambiguous, and precise.

Such detailed guidance belongs in the writers' guide. The writers' guide should present the style and content rules for procedures at a facility. It should be based on the principles in this document, as well as on facility policies. The writers' guide provides the specific information that the procedure writer needs on a daily basis.

Consider another example: this book says that white space should be used to separate steps and substeps in a manner that conveys their hierarchy. The writers' guide would explain exactly how to do that; it might say, *Insert two blank lines (24 points) before a step and one blank line (12 points) before a substep.*

Writers' guides are widely used by procedure writers in the nuclear power industry, particularly for emergency operating procedures, which must meet especially stringent standards. A writers' guide is a good idea at any facility where procedures are written. At a minimum, you should keep a notebook documenting the practices that you follow and disseminate it among your fellow writers.

1.3   About this Book

Two important aspects of procedures are correctness and usability. Technically correct procedures do not contain any errors of fact. Usable procedures present information in a manner that will be understandable and clear to the procedure user. This book concentrates on usability. Technical correctness is certainly critical to procedure quality, but it is well beyond the scope of this book to discuss the technical correctness of all types of procedures.

Organization of this Book

This book is divided into five parts:

- Part One, The Basics, introduces this book and procedure writing in general.

- Part Two, Writing Basic Steps, discusses the basics of procedure writing, dealing with only simple steps. This information is organized into a series of principles that the procedure writer should follow.

- Part Three, Format and Organization, discusses the appearance of procedures. This information is also presented in a series of principles.

- Part Four, Writing Complex Steps, discusses lists, conditional statements, and other more complex types of steps. Again, this information is presented in a series of principles.

- Part Five, Conclusion, summarizes the book by discussing some of the problems that the procedure writer will face in light of the principles presented in Parts Two, Three, and Four.

This is the first chapter in Part One. Chapters 2 and 3, also in Part One, discuss the reading process and the writing process, respectively.

A Word About Procedure Complexity

Because this book was originally written for nuclear power plant procedure writers, it describes writing procedures for the worst possible case. Nuclear power plant procedures govern the operation of complex, technological equipment, sometimes in emergency situations. When writing a simpler procedure for, say, changing a spark plug, it would be unnecessary to adhere to all the principles discussed in this book. The cross-referencing system described in Chapter 19, for example, would be overkill for a simple procedure. Yet, it is surprising how many of the principles in this book do apply to all procedures. If a principle applies only to more complex procedures, that fact will be clearly stated in the discussion of the principle. Otherwise, all principles apply to all procedures.

A Word About Examples

Many of the examples in this book are taken from procedures used in nuclear power plants or related facilities. Thus, they are rather technical and you may not understand them, but don't let that disturb you—we don't fully understand the technical nature of many of the examples we use! The principles we present are largely independent of technical content; for example, a step should always begin with an action verb followed by an object, whether that step is *Open the door* or *Decant the supernate*. So, rather than use absurdly simple examples that we would be certain our entire audience would be familiar with, such as writing a shopping list or mowing the lawn, we elected to use technical procedures that would be representative of the types of procedures that you would be likely to be writing. It isn't necessary to fully understand the content of the example to understand the principle being presented.

Chapter 2

The Reading Process

The previous chapter explained that the purpose of this book is to help you write procedures that are more usable, and discussed usability in a relatively general sense. As you read through the rest of this book, specifically Parts Two, Three, and Four, you will be introduced to the many principles that can make procedures more usable. Before delving into these principles, however, it is useful to discuss why usability is so important. This chapter presents that discussion.

2.1   A Model of the Reading Process

A discussion of usability must center on the reading process. Everything that occurs prior to the point where the procedure is read, such as the writers' research and agonizing over word choice, verification and validation, and even photocopying, has one goal—to ensure that, when reading the procedure, the user performs the task correctly. To perform a task correctly, the procedure user must understand what he has read. Thus, an understanding of the reading process is crucial to presenting usable procedures.

This section presents a model of the reading process.[1] A model is a simplified representation of a process. A model describes what something is like and helps us understand unfamiliar concepts by relating them to familiar, and often simpler, concepts.[2] Once this model is explained, we can show how procedures can help reduce error.

Reading is hard work. Although the theories of what takes place in our mind as we read can vary, all postulate a very complex process. A simplified description of this process includes the following steps:

---

[1]This model was suggested by Jan Spyridakis of the University of Washington's Department of Technical Communication and Michael Wenger of IBM (1990).

[2]This model is presented with apologies to reading researchers, who will realize that we have glossed over many aspects of the reading process, such as the distinction between top-down and bottom-up processing, the role of long- and short-term memory, and so on. For an excellent overview of these issues, see Spyridakis and Wenger (1990).

- Readers must recognize characters (i.e., letters, numbers, and other symbols).

- Readers must recognize and assign meanings to words.

- Readers must use their knowledge of English grammar to recognize how these words form sentences.

- Readers must draw upon information in their memory to understand sentences, paragraphs, and entire documents.

All these tasks require cognitive resources. Cognitive resources represent the attention we can devote to a task such as reading and performing a procedure. We have only so many resources available as we read. In many situations, this is not a problem, because we are so familiar with the reading process that we have automated many of the basic activities required, such as word recognition. However, when a document becomes difficult to read, these basic activities require more resources, and this increased demand may "crowd out" the resources that we would otherwise have devoted to understanding what we read. For example, if the reader encounters an unfamiliar word, he or she momentarily stops, decides what the word means, and then continues reading. In this case, additional resources must be devoted to a process (i.e., word recognition) that is typically automatic. These resources must come from someplace, so perhaps comprehension suffers; the sentence must be re-read because, in sorting out the meaning of a word, the reader has lost his train of thought and must re-read the sentence. Figure 2.1 depicts this situation.

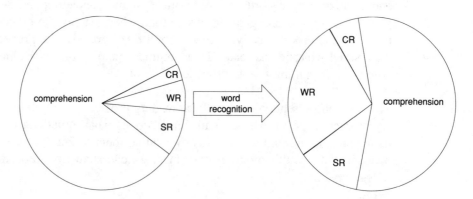

Figure 2.1. Competing Resources. The circle represents the total amount of resources that the reader can devote to reading. On the left, character recognition (CR), sentence recognition (SR), and word recognition (WR) require few resources. The diagram on the right depicts the situation when the reader encounters an unfamiliar word. More resources are required for word recognition, so comprehension receives fewer resources and may suffer.

If you have done your own income taxes (and aren't an accountant), you should be able to easily relate to this phenomenon. Many of us have struggled to understand the instructions provided by the Internal Revenue Service (IRS), and this model neatly explains why this is so. IRS instructions use unfamiliar words or use familiar words in unfamiliar ways. We cannot automate the process of recognizing words and must allocate extra resources to that process. Similarly, the IRS's instructions often include conditional information, which can be difficult to understand, especially when expressed in sentence form (see Chapter 17), so understanding what we read also requires extra resources.

Consider the following passage:

> If a charitable contribution deduction is allowed because of a bargain sale of property to a charitable organization, the adjusted basis for the purposes of determining gain from the sale is the amount which has the same ratio to the adjusted basis as the amount realized has to the fair market value. (Internal Revenue Service, 1990, p. 34)

The reader must not only decide what terms such as *bargain sale* and *adjusted basis* mean, but must also decipher the underlying logic of the sentence. Needless to say, these resources detract from the reader's ability to decide what it all means once he or she grasps the terms and their logic.

The Demands of the Task

This model, as presented thus far, assumes that the reader is concentrating only on the document being read. If he is curled up with a good book, that may well be the case—but if the reader is engaged in any other activity, that activity will also require resources. For example, many people have difficulty reading and watching television at the same time, or reading and carrying on a conversation at the same time. So, when applying this model to the real world, we must take into account factors beyond the document that are vying for the reader's attention.

The procedure reader will always be engaged in at least one other activity—the activity documented in the procedure. Thus, you know that some of the reader's attention will be devoted to the performance of that task and will not be available for reading and understanding the procedure. Figure 2.2 depicts our model in light of these additional demands.

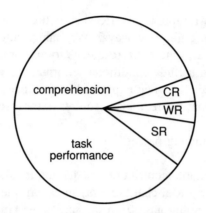

Figure 2.2. Introducing the Demands of a Task. When reading a procedure, the procedure user will also be performing a task. The performance of this task requires resources and reduces the resources that can be allocated to the reading task. In this case character recognition (CR), word recognition (WR), and sentence recognition (SR) require the same amount of resources, so comprehension suffers.

Introducing Stressors

The resources that can be devoted to the reading task are further affected by stressors. Stressors induce stress. Although we are all familiar with the notion of stress, we probably don't consider stress to have both positive and negative effects on performance; it does. Figure 2.3 depicts a stress curve, which relates the level of stress to the likelihood of an error (Kantowitz & Sorkin, 1983). Note how performance suffers at low levels of stress as well as at high levels of stress. At a low level of stress, people are bored and tend not to pay attention, whereas at a high level of stress people may be overloaded and also fail to perform optimally.

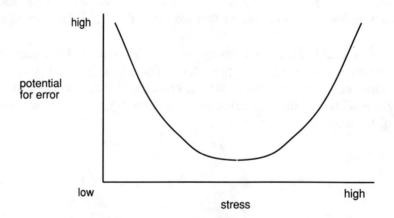

Figure 2.3. Stress Curve. This curve depicts the relationship between the potential for error and stress. At high levels of stress, errors are more likely. At low levels of stress, errors are also likely because workers are bored.

The effects of stress vary from person to person. Some people fall apart under the slightest stress while others appear to thrive on stress. Similarly, different types of stress have different effects on people; for instance, a combat-hardened soldier, who suffers no ill effects under combat, may be terrified of speaking before a group.

An important point to realize, however, is that we *all* have a threshold of stress above which our performance will deteriorate. The analogy to soldiers, in fact, illustrates this. In one study (Berkin, 1964), soldiers were required to perform various tasks in the face of what appeared to be imminent death. In one task, while under artillery fire, a soldier had to follow a procedure for repairing a malfunctioning radio so that he could call the artillery post and tell them to stop firing. The soldiers, who did not know that the artillery was simulated, performed poorly, although soldiers with combat experience fared better. Assessments of soldiers' performance on the battlefield also bear out the effects of stress; only 25 percent will fire effectively against the enemy "unless they are compelled by almost overpowering circumstance or unless all junior leaders constantly 'ride herd' on troops with the specific mission of increasing their fire. The 25 percent estimate stands even for well-trained and campaign-seasoned troops" (Marshall, 1978, p. 50).

Although these are extreme examples, life-threatening incidents are conceivable in situations where procedures are used; examples include emergency procedures in nuclear power plants and, as in the study above, procedures for operating military equipment. Stress can result from other factors as well:

- Workers may be afraid of losing their jobs, or even of doing their jobs poorly.

- A worker may have problems at home.

- A worker may be afraid of looking bad in front of his peers.

- Illness or substance abuse problems may introduce stress.

- Extremes of temperature, noise, or vibration can induce stress (Echeverria et al., 1991).

These factors can introduce stress into the performance of any procedure.

High stress levels reduce the amount of cognitive resources that we can devote to a task—including the reading task. Low stress levels reduce the total amount of cognitive resources that are available; in other words, readers are less likely to pay attention to what they are reading. Figure 2.4 depicts these effects, as well as other demands on the cognitive resources of the procedure user.

Figure 2.4. Competing Resources—The Big Picture.   Stress further reduces the resources that users can devote to a task—in this case, comprehending what is being read. If a reader is under extreme stress, he or she must devote resources to dealing with the stress. If a reader is understressed, resources may be devoted to daydreaming or simply may not be available.

2.2   Applying the Model to Procedures

Recall Figure 2.1, where a reader encountered an unfamiliar word, which required excess resources, reducing the resources that were available for comprehension. Now consider the same situation in our "real world" version of the model in Figure 2.4, where the user who is performing a procedure under stress encounters a sentence that is difficult to understand. Perhaps he is doing his taxes while tired and ill. His resources become overloaded. He can't understand the procedure, perform the task, and deal with the stress all at the same time. Something's got to go. A variety of scenarios are possible:

- The user may decide that the procedure isn't worth the trouble of trying to understand it and thus will discard it. The demands on his resources are reduced, but now an error is more likely because the user no longer has access to important information in the procedure.

- The user may devote more resources to attempting to understand the procedure and devote fewer resources to the task being performed. Because he is paying less attention to what he is doing, an error in task performance becomes more likely. If the procedure user is working with live circuits or around hot machinery, he may even hurt himself.

- The user may continue in the procedure without understanding the word. Again, an error is possible, because he is working without full benefit of the procedure.

Each of these situations is undesirable. As a procedure writer, you cannot do much about the stress the worker is under or the cognitive demands of the task itself, but you can do much to affect the quality of the procedure. By adhering to the guidance in this book, you can make the procedure more usable—and the more usable the procedure is, the fewer cognitive resources it will require. Spyridakis and Wenger (1990, p. 126) sum up the writer's responsibility in this regard:

> Careful writers will lean towards creating documents that, whenever possible, reduce the reader's cognitive load—thus allowing readers to liberate attention for document aspects that cannot be simplified.

As you read through the guidance in here, remember that there will be other factors competing for the procedure user's cognitive resources. Without considering this fact, you may believe that some of the guidance presented here makes a trivial difference in the usability of a procedure. For example, trained users reading the step *Slowly increase flow* (referring to the flow of water through a pipe) will know how slow *slowly* is and are unlikely to make an error. But remember that you are sitting at your desk, under little, if any, stress and not doing anything besides reading this book. The object is not to write a procedure that is usable in this situation, but is usable in an extreme situation. If the user is working in a hot, humid, loud turbine building, rushing to complete a valve line-up so that a reactor can be restarted on schedule, what then?

Remember that low levels of stress can also be a problem. Assume that you are confronted with a wordy step, presented in paragraph form. Again, sitting at your desk, you can probably plod through the step and understand it; but what about a worker on the graveyard shift, working alone and bored? Chances are higher that he will give the step a cursory read, and then do what he thinks it said. Once more, errors become likely. Unmotivated workers will perform better if procedures are easier to understand. Conversely, highly motivated readers can often deal effectively with text that is difficult to read (Spyridakis & Wenger, 1990).

However, if text is too difficult to read, good readers will adopt the habits of poor readers. Spyridakis and Wenger (1990) recount how, when confronted with demanding and unfamiliar technical text, good readers will (1) recall less information; (2) be more likely to read in a list-wise fashion, ignoring cues as to the importance of ideas; (3) distort the meaning of text in their recalls; and (4) have more difficulty applying the information they have read.

By following the guidelines in this book, you will be taking an important step to guard against these effects in procedures.

Chapter 3

The Writing Process

Before the discussion of the specific principles that govern procedure preparation, a brief overview of the procedure writing process may be useful. The procedure writing process is the process that you go through when you revise an existing procedure or write a new procedure from scratch. This chapter discusses that practice. It does not contain any requirements that you must follow; instead, it suggests a process that works for many writers. We encourage you to follow this process, modifying it as necessary so that it works for you.

The procedure writing process consists of five steps:

- Writers begin by *investigating*. They do preliminary research to develop ideas about what they will be writing.

- The next step is to *organize* the thoughts that have been developed. Outlining is a useful organizational tool.

- Once the outline is completed, the next step is to *write* a draft of the procedure.

- Once a draft is written, it should be *revised*.

- When the procedure is finished, it should be *validated and verified*.

It is important to note that these steps are not distinct; they overlap. You may begin one step before the previous step is completed; for instance, you may begin to write before you are finished organizing. This is fine. Some writers cannot completely organize their thoughts until they start writing. Others prefer to have a document fully mapped out before they begin. Adopt an approach that works for you, using these five steps as a general guideline.

3.1   Investigating

When you are writing or revising a procedure, your first step is to ensure that you have the correct technical and usability information on hand to write the procedure—you investigate. There are basically three activities that you perform in this step: reviewing source documentation, interviewing users and subject matter experts, and performing procedure walkdowns.

Reviewing Source Documentation

Procedures typically are based on a variety of technical documents. In technical settings, these may include information provided by vendors, technical specifications, piping and instrumentation diagrams, training materials, administrative procedures, engineering analyses, and other procedures. In other settings they may include memos and management policies. It is important that you gather this material so that you have access to the information that you will need to write an accurate procedure.

If a procedure is being revised, one common error is to use the old procedure as the only source document. The problem with this shortcut is that there is probably no guarantee that the old procedure is correct. If you accept what it says without question, you may be perpetuating errors. In going back to the source documents (and in performing the interviews and walkdowns that are also part of investigating) you can develop an accurate procedure so that the next writer who works on it *can* take credit for your work and will not have to duplicate it.

When dealing with complex procedures, the key to this process, where a procedure writer can take credit for the previous writer's work, is a *technical basis document.* Basis documents present and justify the technical basis for a procedure. A basis document does not have to adhere to any specific form; what is must do is explain why the procedure was written as it was written, referring to source documents as necessary. In complex procedures, such as emergency operating procedures in nuclear reactors, the basis document should include this information for each step. Of course, if a basis document already exists for the procedure, you do not have to go do this work but can use it and add to it for your procedure revision.

In some situations, source documentation may not exist. If this is the case, since you obviously cannot work with what you do not have, the remaining activities in this step, interviews and walkdowns, must provide your technical basis. Once you have completed these interviews and walkdowns, *leave a written record of what you have learned.* Spare the next writer who works on the procedure the trouble that you have been through.

Interviews

Not all of the information you need will be contained in basis documents. Much of it will be in the minds of procedure users and subject matter experts. To get at this information you must talk to these people.

You will typically be interviewing three types of people:

- It is important to talk to procedure users because they are often quite familiar with the technical content of the procedure (including a few tips and hints that never made it into the procedure). Procedure users can also tell you what they want to see in the procedures—and, because they are your customers, this information is important. The discussion of audience analysis in Chapter 8 will return to this point in greater detail.

- You will also talk to technical experts, such as engineers or vendor personnel, who are not procedure users.

- Finally, you may talk with managers, who may outline their expectations for the procedure.

Interviews can be structured or unstructured. In an unstructured interview, you simply call up your buddy on the phone and ask him some questions. These types of contacts can be very valuable. You should devote some effort to developing a network of people within the facility (or with vendors) who you can call when you have a quick question. However, be aware of the danger of relying too much on such a network—you should talk to people who have the answers to your questions, not who are simply easy to reach or do not mind talking to you.

At other times, you may want to take an approach towards interviewing that is more formal. For example, you may be assigned a procedure that you do not know much about, necessitating interviews with people you have never met. In these situations, you probably want to bring a list of prepared questions to the interview and you should concentrate on taking accurate, complete notes. You may even want to record the interview, so long as your subject will not be disturbed by a tape recorder.

Walkdowns

If you have never seen something done, you will have difficulty writing about it. That's why walkdowns are important. You must get out and see what the procedure user must do so that you can describe it in the procedure. Do not confuse this walkdown with the walkdown that will be done when (or if) the procedure is validated and verified. Both walkdowns can be important; this walkdown is a beginning step to get you up to speed on the procedure. During a walkdown, you "act out" all of the steps in the procedure in the location where they will be performed. Walkdowns can provide many types of information. If you are unfamiliar with the procedure, a walkdown can serve as a useful indoctrination to the procedure. Walkdowns can alert you to tasks that will be physically difficult to perform, such as a task that requires users to closely coordinate their activities but is performed in a very loud area. If they cannot hear each other, they may have difficulty coordinating. Walkdowns are also useful for checking the correspondence between equipment labels and the procedure, although it may be too early in the process to worry about that. (But, because the procedure writing steps overlap, you can do a walkdown with a nearly completed draft when it will be useful to check this correspondence.)

It may be useful to combine a walkdown with an interview of a procedure user. The walkdown can remind the interviewee of things he should tell you and give you an idea of what questions to ask.

3.2   Organizing

Before you begin to write, you should have some idea of what you are going to say and how you plan to say it. You have to get organized. Outlining is a good organizational tool—especially in technical writing, including procedures. When you are doing an outline, don't become too concerned with its format. If numbering is helpful, then number the items in the outline. You don't have to use the traditional Roman numeral format that you were probably taught, but you may if you want to.

You may also find it useful to develop a flowchart as you are organizing a procedure, particularly if the procedure contains several alternative courses of action. *Techniques for Preparing Flowchart-Format Emergency Operating Procedures* (Barnes et al., 1989) contains guidance on preparing flowcharts. You may find this report useful; however, remember that it specifically addresses the preparation of flowcharts that are used as procedures and thus contains prescriptive guidance on flowchart format that isn't applicable to a flowchart used only by the procedure writer as an outline.

3.3   Writing the Draft

There is no clear-cut point where you should stop outlining and start writing. As indicated in the introduction to this chapter, different writers begin to write at different points. Some develop complete, meticulous outlines before they begin writing. Others work from a cursory outline. Don't be too concerned with the distinction between the outline and the procedure. Many writers do not distinguish between their outlines and their drafts. Instead, their outline evolves into a finished document. They simply keep fleshing out the outline until it is the document. The point is that, at some point, your document is going to start looking like a procedure.

This technique has been greatly facilitated by the development of word processors. When writers typed, wrote, or even carved in stone, they were restricted to a basically linear process. For the most part, they had to write words in the order they would be read. Not so with the word processor—the writer can skip around the document, leaving ideas half finished, with plans to complete them later, leaving notes to himself that will later be erased, shuffling sections around, and so on. With the word processor, you have much more flexibility in the way you write. Consider your writing habits; are you using this flexibility? Word processors offer much more than spell checking and fancy fonts.

Writer's block is one of the biggest obstacles to getting work done. Sometimes, the best technique for overcoming writer's block is to simply sit down and force yourself to write something, anything. You can always revise and change it later. Other times, writer's block is a symptom of too many distractions. Try getting to work early or staying late, and see if working at times when you are free from distraction is helpful.

The *Handbook of Technical Writing* (Brusaw, Alred, & Oliu, 1987, p. 719) provides additional advice on avoiding writer's block:

- Set up your writing area with the equipment and materials (paper, dictionary, source books, and so forth) you will need to keep going once you get started.

- Use whatever writing tools—separately or in combination—are most comfortable for you: pencil, felt-tip pen, typewriter, word processor, or whatever.

- Remind yourself that you are beginning a version of your writing project that no one else will read.

- Remember the writing projects you've finished in the past—you have completed something before, and you will this time.

- Start with the section that seems easiest to you—your reader will not know or care that you first wrote a section in the middle.

- Give yourself a time limit (10 or 15 minutes, for example) in which you will keep your pen or fingers on the typewriter moving, regardless of how good or bad your writing seems to you. The point is to keep moving.

- Don't let anything stop you when you are rolling along easily—if you stop and come back, you may not regain the momentum.

- But stop writing before you're completely exhausted; when you begin again, you may be able to regain your momentum.

- When you finish a section, give yourself a small reward—a short walk, a cup of coffee, a chat with a friend, an easy task, and so on.

With some writers, writer's block is a sign that there is something wrong with what they are trying to say. So, if you find yourself blocked, consider what you are writing. Do you know what you want to say? Is it logical? Are you saying what procedure users will want to know? Is there an underlying technical problem?

3.4   Revising

Once you have completed a draft, it is time to revise it. Just as there is no clear-cut line between outlining and writing, there is no such line between writing and revising. Most writers revise as they write. However, at some point, you will have completed the procedure and will be ready to read through it again, enhance it, and correct any errors.

Ideally, you should set the procedure aside for a few days before you revise. The break will allow you to approach revision with a clear mind. You will be able to see problems and discrepancies that were not apparent to you when you were writing. Although the schedules under which writers work frequently may not allow this time, you should make every effort possible to give yourself a break between writing the draft and revising it.

Keep the writers' guide and this book close at hand as you are revising. You should check for all types of problems, from global (is the procedure accurate?) to specific (are words spelled correctly?). Procedure writing is very detail-oriented, and this is the stage where you will be checking the details. Take the time to check and double-check everything. Don't let things slide with the expectation that they will be caught during validation and verification. Try to pass off a procedure that is as accurate as possible.

3.5   Validating and Verifying

The best way to improve your writing is to have others review and comment on it. In the nuclear power industry, this process is formally known as validation and verification. It can be helpful for many forms of procedures. At some nuclear facilities, validation and verification are considered two separate processes; at others, they are considered to be the same process. Here, we will use the term *validation* to refer to both processes.

During validation, a procedure is assessed to determine whether it meets the following criteria:

- The procedure should successfully direct users to accomplish its objective.

- The procedure should be usable.

- The procedure should be accurate.

- The procedure should be written in accordance with the appropriate standards (e.g., the writers' guide).

- The procedure should be written at the appropriate level of detail (i.e., it should present all important information without presenting superfluous information).

- The equipment labels and markings cited in the procedure should correspond with actual hardware.

Validation consists of desk-top reviews of procedures, walkdowns of procedures, simulator exercises, and observed execution of procedures. The exact nature of the validation of a particular procedure will depend on several factors, such as the consequences of an error in procedure execution, the availability of a simulator, the users' familiarity with the procedure, and so on. It is important that all procedures undergo at least minimal validation.

Part Two:
Writing Basic Steps

Chapter 4

Introduction: Writing Basic Steps

Beginning with Chapter 5, this book will present a series of principles that guide effective procedure writing. This chapter introduces the collection of principles in Part Two that pertain to writing basic action steps. These principles apply to simple procedures as well as complex procedures.

Steps are the heart of the procedure—they tell users what to do. In fact, the characteristic that most strongly separates procedures from other forms of writing is that information in procedures is presented in steps. In most other forms of writing, information is presented in paragraphs. In procedures, information is typically broken into smaller chunks (Zimmerman & Campbell, 1988). Berry (1981, p. 22) explains why:

> Narrative formats use sentences and paragraphs to separate the steps of a procedure. Sometimes steps are also separated by commas within sentences. Many narrative formats for procedures are ineffective. This format encourages writers to include a lot of unnecessary description and padding. Narrative formats are also more demanding of the user—the narrative steps of a procedure do not stand out clearly.

Wright and Reid (1973) have conducted experiments that have shown the superiority of steps over the narrative format. A comparison of Figures 4.1 and 4.2 demonstrates the superiority of steps over a narrative format for procedures.

Cut the air filters into 1-2 cm^2 pieces and place the filter pieces into the nickel crucibles. Ash the mixture. Pipette 1 ml of strontium carrier and 1 ml of calcium carrier into the ash. Note that 15 gm of NaOH are required when analyzing 1-5 air filters of smears. Add 5 gm of NaOH pellets for each 1 gm of ash and add 5 gm of NaOH in excess. Be aware that the fusion process will likely result in a splatter that may cause personnel injury, loss of sample, or both unless protective gear is used. Fuse the sample in a nickel-covered nickel crucible.

Figure 4.1. Narrative Procedure. Compare this figure with series of steps presented in Figure 4.2.

[1]   Cut the air filters into 1-2 cm^2 pieces.   ___

[2]   Place the filter pieces into the nickel crucibles.   ___

[3]   Ash the mixture.   ___

[4]   Pipette 1 ml of strontium carrier and 1 ml of calcium carrier into the ash.   ___

NOTE   *15 gm of NaOH are required when analyzing 1-5 air filters of smears.*

[5]   Add 5 gm of NaOH pellets for each 1 gm of ash and add 5 gm of NaOH in excess.   ___

****
WARNING

The fusion process will likely result in a splatter that may cause personnel injury, loss of sample, or both unless protective gear is used.
****

[6]   Fuse the sample in a nickel-covered nickel crucible.   ___

Figure 4.2. Step-by-Step Procedure. Here, the information is presented in steps (and a note and a caution). Errors are less likely in this format because the actions are clearly differentiated from each other.

This part of this book, Part Two, will discuss how basic steps should be written. It concentrates on the content of steps rather then the format. Part Three will discuss format. Part Four will then discuss more complex forms of steps.

This part contains five chapters (in addition to this chapter):

- Chapter 5 discusses step syntax—the way steps are actually written. Steps should conform to the rules of English grammar; they should be written as imperatives (i.e., begin with an action verb); and they should be simple, concise, positive statements.

- Chapter 6 discusses vocabulary and word choice in procedures. Simple words are preferable to complex words; consistency is also important.

- Chapter 7 discusses punctuation.

- Chapter 8 discusses level of detail. Procedures that contain too much detail will be cluttered and difficult to use, while procedures that contain too little detail can contribute to errors.

- Chapter 9 discusses the presentation of numerical information in procedures.

Chapter 5

Step Syntax

Syntax is the way in which words are arranged. This chapter discusses the syntax of action steps. It presents five principles:

- Follow the rules of English grammar unless there is a very good reason not to do so.

- Use sentences that are as short as possible in steps.

- Write steps that are concise, but not telegraphic.

- Use the active voice.

- Write steps as positive commands.

5.1 Follow the rules of English grammar unless there is a very good reason not to do so.

Summary

Procedures that are not written according to the rules of accepted English grammar, through either error or intention, may be misunderstood because they violate the expectations that readers bring to documents. Even if grammatical errors do not lead readers to misunderstand the procedure, they can lessen the procedure's credibility in the eyes of the user.

Discussion

The word *grammar* actually has two related meanings, as explained by Brusaw, Alred, and Oliu (1987, p. 273):

> Grammar is a systematic description of the way words work together to form a coherent language; in this sense, it is an explanation of the structure of a language. However, grammar is popularly taken to mean the set of "rules" that governs how a language ought to be spoken or written. . . .

Here, we consider the second definition of grammar—the rules that govern the correct usage of a language.

The Importance of Following the Rules of Grammar

The grammar used in procedures should be very restricted; for example, steps may be written only as imperative sentences (see Section 5.4). However, few (if any) of these restrictions contradict the established rules of English grammar. It is important that procedures adhere to these rules, because readers expect to see documents that adhere to grammatical convention and may be confused by deviations and because ungrammatical writing may be viewed as unprofessional and flawed.

In *Modern American Usage*, Follett (1966, p. 23) portrays grammar as a sort of referee in the game of writing:

> When instinct fails, grammar helps by naming the fault and the remedy. . . . Anyone is free to dissent, but the rebels are likely to find that the convenience won by anarchy can become terribly inconvenient. Such opportunism has all the disadvantages of changing signals without consultation or the rules of the game without foreseeing all of the consequences.

Simon (1980, pp. 203-204) explains why it is important to adhere to the established conventions of grammar:

> There is, of course, the fundamental matter of courtesy to the other person, but it goes beyond that: why waste time on unscrambling simple meaning when there are more complex questions that should receive our *undivided attention*? [emphasis added]

Simon's concern reflects a central theme of this book. The reader of a procedure must, under the best of conditions, divide his or her attention among many tasks. Why add more distractions by deviating from standard grammatical conventions? Adhering to established grammatical conventions helps the reader comprehend and remember information because doing so frees up cognitive resources that might otherwise be needed to work through grammatical puzzles.

Further, correct grammar, like correct spelling, makes our writing more credible. Procedures must sell themselves to their users and, like all documents, they are sometimes judged on characteristics that may seem superficial. For instance, misspelled words are seldom mangled so severely that the reader does not realize which word was intended. So why worry about misspellings? Our audience can figure out what we meant.

We worry because we are making the reader figure out what the word is and because a misspelled word *looks* bad. Too many misspellings are seen as an indication of sloppiness; and if the writer is sloppy about something as basic as spelling, the reader can no longer be certain that the writer was not sloppy with some of the more substantial matters, like checking his facts.

In the same way, the step *Ensure that a safety injection have actuated* may be perfectly understandable, but the user who recognizes the error is likely to think less of the procedure writer and of the procedure itself. (The step should say, *Ensure that a safety injection has actuated*.) He may wonder whether anyone validated and verified the procedure and what other, more serious mistakes may be lying in wait for him. So, procedure writers should avoid anything that will undermine the procedure, which is exactly what grammatical errors do.

Some *Basic* Grammatical Terminology

We all have taken grammar courses at some point in our lives, perhaps in high school, and most likely disliked the experience and found it of no benefit in later life. And, the fact is, there is no evidence that knowledge of grammar makes us better or worse writers:

> It is quite possible to write adequately without knowing a single thing about grammar (or at least without knowing a single thing that is taught under the heading of "grammar" in the public schools). Furthermore, knowing a whole lot about grammar is not likely to make you an excellent writer. In fact, one survey after another has shown that formal study of grammar in school has no correlation whatsoever with ability to write effectively. So why bother? (Stratton, 1984, p. 377)

We bother because an overview of grammar provides a common ground for discussing procedure writing. Or, as Follett (1966, p. 25) says, "Like the carpenter or plumber, the writer cannot carry on his own trade without technical terms." When the writers' guide says to begin an action step with a verb, a procedure writer should know what a verb is. Hence, this section will define some basic grammatical terms, beginning with some basic parts of speech. (If you are familiar with grammar, you will realize that this section generalizes and simplifies the topic a great deal.)

- A *noun* is a person, place, or thing. In the sentence *John saw the tree*, *John* and *tree* are nouns.

- A *verb* denotes action or state of being. In the sentence *John saw the tree*, *saw* is a verb, as it explains the action that John is taking. In the sentence *John is happy*, *is* is a verb, because it denotes John's state of being.

- Some sentences use *auxiliary verbs*, also known as helping verbs. Auxiliary verbs indicate mood, voice, and tense. In *The tree was seen by John*, *was* is an auxiliary verb.

- *The*, *a*, and *an* are *articles*. Articles modify nouns by indicating whether they should have a restricted or general meaning. In *John saw the tree*, the article *the* indicates that John saw a specific tree. The sentence *John saw a tree* refers to no tree in particular.

- *Adverbs* modify verbs. (To remember this, think that adverbs add to verbs.) In *John slowly ran*, *slowly* is an adverb. Most adverbs end in *-ly*.

- *Adjectives* modify nouns. In *John saw the big tree*, *big* is an adjective.

These parts of speech are combined into phrases, clauses, and sentences:

- A *phrase* is a group of two or more words that does not contain a subject and a verb. *The tree* is a phrase.

- A *clause* is a group of two or more words that contains a subject and a verb. A clause can be a sentence; *John saw the tree* is a clause. Such clauses are called *independent* clauses, because they can stand independently. Other clauses, such as *While John watched the tree*, are not sentences. These are *dependent clauses*, because they depend on the sentence to which they belong for meaning (e.g., *While John watched the tree, Tom cut it down*).

- A *sentence* consists of one or more clauses, at least one of which must be an independent clause.

Sentences consist of subjects, verbs, and objects. Grammatical terminology overlaps here; subjects, verbs, and objects can be phrases or clauses. The terms *subject*, *verb*, and *object* are ways of classifying the phrases and clauses that appear within sentences.

- The *subject* answers the question who or what is performing the action expressed by the verb. In *John saw the tree*, *John* is the subject. Subjects are nouns or phrases acting as nouns. In the *imperative* sentences that comprise procedure steps, the subject is the omitted word *you*; for example, in *Open the valve*, the subject is *you*, as in *You open the valve*.

- The *verb* expresses the action in the sentence. A verb (used in this context) can be a verb or a phrase acting as a verb.

- The *object* receives the action of a sentence. Objects are nouns or noun phrases. In *Open the valve*, *the valve* is the object.

Two Common Errors

A complete discussion of grammatical errors is well beyond the scope of this section. However, a discussion of one common error (subject-verb disagreement) and one intentional practice (omission of articles or auxiliary verbs) that compromise grammar in procedures will serve as an indication of the types of problems that might arise.

Subjects and verbs must agree in number; usually, we make subjects and verbs agree in our writing without really thinking about it. We write *The dogs are back* and *The dog is back* without much difficulty. Subject-verb disagreements typically arise in more complex sentences, where the subject is separated from the verb. For instance, we may write *A census of all fifty states are quite an undertaking*, mistakenly allowing the plural *states*, which is closer to the verb than the subject *census*, to determine the form of the verb. The correct version of the sentence is *A census of all fifty states is quite an undertaking (i.e., census . . . is).*

Errors of this type can occur in procedures. Consider Figure 5.1. At first glance, the step in Figure 5.1 appears to be correct. However, it should read *Ensure that one of the following pumps is in service* (i.e., *one . . . is*). The danger is that users may base their interpretation of the step on the verb and mistakenly believe that both pumps should be placed in service. With the use of the correct verb, this danger is lessened.

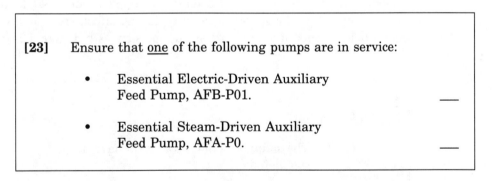

Figure 5.1. Subject-Verb Disagreement in a Procedure. The subject-verb disagreement in this step may be difficult to detect at first glance—the verb should be *is*. It is a potential source of user error, however, because users may key on the verb *are* and think that they may place *both* pumps in service.

Sometimes, procedure writers deliberately violate the rules of grammar in the interest of brevity, omitting words that they feel contribute little to the sentence. The example that will be considered here is omission of articles and auxiliary verbs.

Articles (i.e., *a*, *an*, and *the*) indicate whether a noun is intended in a general or a specific sense. As such, they provide important information to readers. Yet, somehow, the notion has evolved in some forms of writing, procedures included, that prose flows better without articles. According to *Words into Type* (1974, p. 372), articles "are often misused and are often omitted without reason." This tendency may be carried to an extreme in procedures. We would never write *I went to store*, yet many procedure writers do not hesitate to write *Ensure that all of following criteria are met*.

Articles provide subtle clues to meaning in prose. The difference between *We were met at the Dublin airport by the officials of the Irish Republic* and *We were met at the Dublin airport by officials of the Irish Republic* is that the first implies that the visitors were met by *all* officials of the Irish Republic, while the second implies that the visitors were met by *some* officials of the Irish Republic (Follett, 1966, p. 37). While it is true that, in procedures, we cannot trust the communication of information solely to the subtle clues provided by articles, it is not a wise idea to discard all articles as useless. Readers expect to see articles, and may be confused by their absence. Because articles are such short words, there is simply very little cost to including them in procedures, while the risk of excluding them is that a step may be misunderstood.

A similar case can be made for auxiliary verbs. Why write *Ensure safety injection actuated* when *Ensure safety injection has actuated* is clearer and reads more smoothly, and at only the cost of adding a three-letter word. While in this example the loss of the article has a rather jarring effect, procedure writers often omit articles when a list format breaks up the step, as in Figure 5.2.

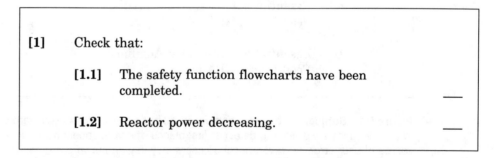

[1]   Check that:

      [1.1]   The safety function flowcharts have been completed.   —

      [1.2]   Reactor power decreasing.   —

Figure 5.2. Omitted Auxiliary Verb in a List. Although the error is not immediately apparent here, the item should read, *Reactor power is decreasing*; otherwise, the step says, *Check that reactor power decreasing*.

Auxiliary verbs indicate mood and voice, which are not particularly applicable to procedures, and tense, which is applicable to procedures:

- Mood can be indicative or subjunctive. The indicative mood expresses a fact. The subjunctive mood expresses a possibility. In *If I were a rich man* the auxiliary verb *were* makes the clause subjunctive, indicating that the notion of becoming a rich man is an unlikely possibility.

- Voice can be first, second, or third person. Different auxiliary verbs are used in the following statements: *I am coming, You are coming,* and *He is coming.*

- Tense indicates time, either past, present, or future.

The critical issue for articles in procedures is the conveyance of tense. There is a difference between *Check that reactor power is decreasing* and *Check that reactor power has been decreasing,* and the auxiliary verbs convey this information.

5.2   Use sentences that are as short as possible in steps.

Summary

As a general rule, the sentences in procedure steps should be as short as possible, but understandability should never be compromised when a sentence is shortened. A short sentence containing one long clause may be more difficult to understand than a long sentence containing several short clauses.

Discussion

It has long been recognized that shortening sentences can be an effective way to improve the readability of a document. Chall (1984) writes that, after vocabulary, sentence length has the greatest effect on readability. In fact, most readability formulas, which measure how hard a passage is to read, rely primarily on the average length of sentences and the average length of words to determine the complexity of the writing.

Short sentences are not a goal in themselves, however—understandable writing is the goal. A consideration of sentence length should therefore be tempered with an understanding of the other factors that affect readability and an understanding that a short sentence is not automatically an understandable sentence.

It is not uncommon to encounter rules in technical communication that specify a maximum (or optimal) sentence length. Huckin (1983) warns against relying too heavily on these rules. He recounts an amusing story of a colleague who had a student whose writing

> was "incontrovertibly soporific." It turned out that the student had once been told by his eighth-grade English teacher that "the average American sentence contained eighteen words," and he thereafter devoted his writing

life to producing eighteen-word sentences! Indeed, [Huckin's colleague] counted the words and sentences in one of his papers and found that of the thirty-eight sentences in it, thirty-six were eighteen words long (the two others were seventeen and nineteen words long)! (p. 103)

Huckin is obviously presenting an extreme instance here, but he makes a valid point—sentence-length requirements can be useful, but only as guidelines. Long sentences may be more difficult to understand than short sentences, but this is not necessarily so and the clarity of a sentence should never be compromised simply to shorten it.

Further, the guideline to use short sentences is probably an oversimplification. Through a series of experiments, Coleman (1963) demonstrated that clause length, rather than sentence length, affects readability. He compared shorter sentences, such as *A detailed knowledge of the lower Mississippi valley would be quite helpful* with longer versions that contained shorter clauses, such as *If you knew the lower Mississippi valley in detail, it would be quite helpful.* He found that sentences such as the second were easier to understand, and attributed the difference to clause length. He writes (1963, pp. 340-341),

> Thus it seems that the advice to prefer short sentences might be better rephrased as a rule to prefer short clauses. If the clauses in a writer's composition are short, he will probably not improve readability much by emphasizing the boundaries between them with periods and capitals.

5.3   Write steps that are concise, but not telegraphic.

Summary

Write concisely, but do not violate established grammatical conventions by writing in a telegraphic style.

Discussion

Concise writing has long been recognized as good writing. In *The Elements of Style*, Strunk and White (1979, p. 23) write,

> A sentence should contain no unnecessary words, a paragraph no unnecessary sentences for the same reason that a drawing should have no unnecessary lines and a machine no unnecessary parts. This requires not that the writer make all his sentences short, or that he avoid all detail and treat his subjects only in outline, but that every word tell.

The Handbook of Technical Writing (Brusaw, Alred, & Oliu, 1987, p. 122) offers similar advice: "Careful writers remove every word, phrase, clause, or sentence they can without sacrificing clarity."

Writing should be pruned with care, however. There are many shortcuts often naively taken by writers who recognize the need for conciseness but who are not sensitive to the nuances of meaning that adherence to standard grammatical conventions help to ensure. Many of these shortcuts lead to a telegraphic writing style. A telegraphic writing style eliminates words here and there and makes the reader do the work of filling in the gaps. Often the reader can successfully fill in all of the gaps, but the cost in terms of the cognitive resources required to do so will almost always outweigh the advantages of the trivial reduction in length created. Further, there is always the risk that the reader will fill in the gaps incorrectly.

The fallacy of a telegraphic writing style can be seen by taking it to its logical extreme. Writers who use this style leave out words that the reader should be able to fill in. Thus the reader is supplied with subjects, main verbs, objects, adjectives, and adverbs and asked to fill in most of the rest of the sentence elements, such as prepositions, articles, conjunctions, and auxiliary verbs. Prior to the invention of paper, writers sometimes omitted even more from their texts simply because the physical task of writing was so difficult. For example, some ancient stone manuscripts contain no vowels. Such extreme omissions often do not prevent a reader from deciphering a text. Consider, for example, the following passage where all articles, prepositions, conjunctions, auxiliary verbs and most vowels have been omitted: *Xpml xtreme telagrphc wrtng. Artcls prpostions xiliary vrbs mst vls absnt.* With some work this passage can be read. Adding the vowels and essential punctuation to the passage helps, but reading the passage still requires considerable effort: *Example extreme telegraphic writing. Articles, prepositions, auxiliary verbs, most vowels absent.* The addition of vowels and punctuation only marginally improves the text. However, the addition of the missing words provides for a passage where the meaning can be derived with minimal effort: *This is an example of extreme telegraphic writing. The articles, prepositions, auxiliary verbs, and most of the vowels are absent.*

This example is not as farfetched as it may seem. When combined with the excessive use of acronyms and abbreviations, a telegraphic writing style in procedures can produce text as cryptic as the first example above. Given, then, that it is unacceptable to leave out of the text everything that the reader should be able to figure out, what can the writer leave out to achieve conciseness? Section 5.1 would suggest that the answer to this question might be "nothing," as leaving out sentence elements is almost bound to result in a violation of some grammatical convention. However, this extreme position is not quite true. Some things can be left out of some passages; for example, some abbreviations and acronyms (which omit many letters from words) can be used. However, the first and most effective step towards concise writing is not to figure out what words (or other elements) can be pulled from a passage but to find the way of expressing the information that is the most concise (in terms of both step length and clause length). For example, the example above contains two relatively short clauses and may be preferable to the single clause rendering: *As an example of extreme telegraphic writing, in this passage the articles, prepositions, auxiliary verbs, and most of the values are absent.*

Once the most concise presentation has been found, the passage may be made more concise through the judicious use of abbreviations and acronyms and by removing certain words. A necessary condition for removing any word is that the word removed is not essential for the reader to understand the text. However, this is not a sufficient condition because, as the above examples demonstrate, words that facilitate comprehension (even though they may not be necessary for comprehension) still aid the reader. Grammatically required words can be omitted, however, if they are both unnecessary and their presence actually impedes communication. To ensure effective communication and consistency in procedures, special care should be taken whenever violations of established conventions are considered and the specific cases should be codified in the writers' guide used by procedure writers.

5.4   Use the active voice.

Summary

Write action instructions as imperatives in the active voice.

Discussion

There are a number of reasons for using the active voice (e.g., *read this*) rather than the passive voice (e.g., *this should be read*) in procedures. Procedures differ from other types of writing, where there can be good reason to use the passive voice. Mixing active and passive sentences can introduce sentence variety, which in turn can make a document more pleasurable to read. (Providing sentence variety is not a good goal for procedure writers, who should focus on consistency rather than variety.) Also, in conventional prose, it may occasionally be appropriate to use the passive voice to emphasize the object of a verb rather than the performer of the action. However, as pointed out by Porter (1991), most of the apparent advantages of the passive voice in technical documents are illusionary and the use of the passive voice will in fact undermine the tone of a document, force the writer to use long complex sentences, render the writing "immediately forgettable," and bore readers to tears (p. 88). Porter's tongue-in-cheek essay on the advantages of the passive voice, however, barely begins to identify its major weaknesses.

If all other things are equal, the active voice is preferable to the passive voice because the active voice more closely matches the way people remember and process information. However, all other things are seldom equal and, in fact, the active voice tends to promote a number of recognized good writing practices (Coleman, 1963). For example, the active voice tends to promote the use of "personal words" (e.g., *I, you*) as subjects and objects making text more memorable. Active sentences tend to be shorter than passives (Coleman, 1963; Porter, 1991; Anderson, 1991). Anderson correctly states that the active voice allows "you to speak directly to readers, telling them as briefly as possible what to do" (p. 661). Figure 5.3 shows how the active voice can shorten steps.

Passive	Active
The operator then sets the dial to 7.	Set the dial to 7.
The parts should be cleaned with oil.	Clean the parts with oil.

Figure 5.3. Use of the Active Voice. Instructions using the active voice are more concise and easier to understand.

The active voice also gives procedures more authority (Lannon, 1991) and focuses steps on actors and actions (Anderson, 1991). The subject of an imperative in the active voice is *you*, the performer of the action. The word *you* is omitted because it is so readily understood. The verb showing the action is then placed prominently as the initial word in the sentence. Thus, the sentence *Clean the parts with oil* focuses on the subject of the sentence (you) and the action you are to perform (clean). By contrast, *The parts should be cleaned with oil* treats the object of the action (the parts) as the subject of the sentence and leaves the actor vague—whether you or someone else should clean the parts is not clear. The verb is buried in the middle of the sentence, where it is more likely to be forgotten than if it were placed either at the beginning or the end of the sentence.

Most of the issues discussed above, while important, are somewhat indirect consequences of using the passive voice. When the direct effects of the use of the active and passive voices are considered, the value of the active voice becomes even more evident. Passive sentences clearly place higher cognitive demands upon readers than do actives. Slobin (1966) found that subjects took longer to identify whether statements were true or false when the sentences were written in the passive voice rather than the active voice. Herriot (1969) found that subjects also took longer to identify the logical subjects and objects in passive constructions for certain types of sentences when those sentences were cast in the passive voice.

Most importantly, sentences written in the active voice are remembered better than sentences written in the passive voice, and at least some passive sentences are remembered as active sentences (Coleman, 1963; Anderson, 1963). For example, it has been shown that people will recall a previously read passive sentence such as *The mouse was chased by the cat* as an active sentence (*The cat chased the mouse*) and believe that they initially read the sentence in the active form. There are two important implications of this research finding. First, readers will need to devote substantially more attention and cognitive resources to the task of reading passive sentences than they would active sentences. When reading passive sentences, an additional complex task is added to the reading process—the task of recoding the information into active constructions. Second, any intended advantage of using the passive voice is likely to be lost, because readers will translate the text into the active voice and process the information as if it were written in the active voice anyway. Thus, there appear to be many disadvantages to using the passive voice in procedures and few, if any, advantages.

5.5   Write steps as positive commands.

Summary

Write action instructions as positive statements, although concise, nonambiguious negative statements are sometimes appropriate.

Discussion

Follett (1966, p. 223) warns, "For many reasons, negative statements have to skirt more grammatical pitfalls than do positive statements." Other authorities and many researchers also warn against use of negative statements. There is substantial evidence to suggest that people do prefer to deal with positive information rather than negative information.

Ensure the valve is not open is a negative statement. *Ensure the valve is closed* is a corresponding positive statement. All else being equal, readers will find it easier to understand the positive statement (Sherman, 1973). Thus, in this particular situation, it is preferable to write *closed* rather than *not open*. A statement containing more than one negation can bring a reader to his knees—*IF the valve is NOT open, THEN do not adjust flow*. These should be avoided at all times.

However, prescriptions to write positive statements are like the prescription to write short sentences that was debunked in Section 5.2. You should avoid negatives, but negative statements are not always harder to understand simply because they are negative. Negative sentences might be more difficult to understand because they tend to be wordier; in the first example above, the negative statement (*Ensure the valve is not open*) is six words long while the positive statement is five words long. Some negative statements also tend to be inherently vague (Sherman, 1973; Harbaugh, 1991). The reader must determine by exclusion what is true; if someone is not happy, then is he sad? Such determinations take effort and introduce the potential for misunderstanding.

Such limitations do not hold true for all negative statements, however. Negative statements can be quite emphatic (Burnett, 1990) and a concise, nonambiguous negative statement can communicate quite effectively. Consider *Do not touch the live wires or you may be electrocuted.* Attempt to rewrite the sentence and it loses some of its punch; *Avoid touching live wires. . .* is not as forceful and *Live wires should not be touched . . .* is an ambiguous passive.

You should in general avoid using negative statements in your procedures, but do not banish them all without consideration. When you do use a negative statement, ensure that it is concise and unambiguous. You should also be aware of several pitfalls in the use of negatives.

Negating words, such as *not*, should be placed with care and you should carefully consider what exactly is being negated. The sentence *All of these acids are not found in protein foods* "flirts with the meaning" that no acids are found in any protein foods (Follett, 1966, p. 223). If the author means that some acids may be found in protein foods, a clearer rewrite would be *Not all of these acids are found in protein foods.* All negatives introduce the potential for this kind of misunderstanding.

Negatives may be useful to "suggest the gray area of meaning between the negative and the positive" (Brusaw, Alred, & Oliu, 1987, p. 202). For instance, *not hot* does not mean the same thing as *cold*; something that is lukewarm is neither hot nor cold. Such constructions should be used with care in procedures, however, which are no place to be introducing subtle shades of meaning. You should also be careful, whenever you use a negative, that any gray area of meaning that might be implied will not introduce confusion. It is worthy to note, though, that in this example the gray area of meaning stems as much from the use of the word *cold* as from the negation. If a specific temperature were used instead, for example, *not above 40°F*, the potential for confusion would be reduced. Even better, of course, would be to say, *40°F or below*, eliminating the negation as well as the vague term.

Chapter 6

Vocabulary

Vocabulary refers to word choice. It is important that procedures use words that are easy to understand and convey correct meaning. It is also important that words be used consistently. This chapter presents several principles regarding vocabulary in procedures:

- Use words consistently within and among procedures.

- Use short, simple words that are common in standard American English.

- Avoid words that may be misunderstood.

- Restrict the use of abbreviations and acronyms.

6.1 Use words consistently within and among procedures.

Summary

Words and phrases should be used consistently within and among procedures so that users will not attribute differences in meaning to spurious differences in presentation. A restrictive list of action verbs should be developed.

Discussion

One of the most important differences between technical writing (including procedure writing) and other forms of writing is the importance of consistency.

"Once you've started referring to something by a particular name, *continue* referring to it that way," Huckin (1983, p. 101) writes. "Don't vary your terminology simply for the sake of variation."

Farkas and Farkas (1981, p. 6) expand on the need for consistency:

> Every manuscript contains mechanical elements of numerous kinds: abbreviations, hyphenated compounds, numerals, spelled numbers, and so forth. The editor [and writer] must ensure that throughout the manuscript these recurring elements are treated consistently, that is, in a uniform or else logical and harmonious way. The human mind has an inherent need for order, and if these elements are not treated consistently, the reader may perceive the document to be disorderly and unprofessional and may be distracted by the inconsistencies. Worse still, in some instances, the inconsistent treatment of mechanical elements can be genuinely confusing, because the reader may assume that two treatments of the same thing indicate some distinction in meaning that the reader has failed to understand.

Consistency is particularly important in procedures, which tend to be terse and concise, requiring each word to convey substantial information.

As action verbs are fundamental to the meaning of a step, special effort should be taken to ensure that they are used consistently. An action verb is (typically) the first word in a simple action step; it specifies the action that is to be taken. In *Open the valve*, *open* is the action verb. A list of action verbs should be developed and only verbs from this list should be used in procedures. Each verb should be clearly defined and the list should be carefully edited to eliminate redundancy so that, for instance, users do not have to guess at the meaning of such similar verbs as *ensure*, *assure*, and *check*. Further, because users frequently give oral instructions based on procedures, verbs that sound alike but have different meanings should be avoided; for example, *reduce* is preferable to *decrease*, which sounds like *increase*.

Consistency applies to all vocabulary in procedures. Equipment nomenclature should also be presented consistently. A piece of equipment should not be identified by its common name at one place in the procedure and by its assigned number later in the procedure. Cross-referencing terms and conditional terms should also be used consistently.

These consistency requirements apply to phrases as well as words. Certain key phrases will be used repeatedly in procedures. For example, *Continue in this procedure* may be used to indicate that the user may continue in the procedure before the present step is completed; this phrase should not be used interchangeably with *Proceed from this step* or even *Continue on in this procedure*.

If users will be dealing with multiple procedures, especially if the same people will be using different procedures, consistency between procedures can be as important as consistency within a procedure. Consistent presentation also simplifies the work of procedure writers and validators and verifiers. Obviously, if there are discrete sets of procedure users and writers for some classes of procedures, the need for inter-procedure consistency is not as strong.

Consistency is ensured through a combination of activities. A detailed writers' guide must set standards for consistency and must be used by procedure writers. Validators and verifiers must be aware of standards for consistency and must take the time and effort to ensure that the procedure is consistent. This is not the most exciting of tasks. Checking for consistency can be a meticulous, dull process; yet it is important. The fewer people that review for consistency the better. Having a pool of 5 or 10 people who review for consistency is a somewhat self-defeating process, as inconsistencies among reviewers will contribute to inconsistencies.

6.2   Use short, simple words that are common in standard American English.

Summary

Words must be understandable. Use the simplest, most common word possible that accurately conveys your intended meaning and is consistent with other word usage in the procedure.

Discussion

The English language includes many words that are synonymous (i.e., mean the same thing). To choose one of many examples, the words *heroism*, *courage*, and *bravery* mean much the same thing. When choosing among a group of words that mean approximately the same thing, the procedure writer is guided by concerns of accuracy, consistency, and understandability.

Accuracy is critical. Words must accurately convey their intended meaning. The English language is rife with subtle shades of meaning. While the words *inexpensive* and *cheap* can generally be considered to be synonymous, their connotations are very different; if you buy an inexpensive car, you have gotten a good deal, but if you buy a cheap car, it is likely to break down and give you trouble. Any attempt to universally substitute *inexpensive* for *cheap* (or visa versa) could easily change the meaning of a document. So, when considering issues of consistency and understandability, you must always ensure that the word *says* what you mean.

That said, it is important that words be used consistently. Differences in word choice should denote differences in meaning, not a desire to introduce some variety. Consistency was discussed in Section 6.1.

It is also important to use the most understandable word that accurately and consistently conveys the meaning you intend. Complex vocabulary has a strong effect on readability:

> The research in readability has uncovered over one hundred factors related to difficulty—such factors as vocabulary, sentences, ideas, concepts, text organization, content, abstractness, appeal, format, and illustrations. Of these factors, the two found consistently to be the most strongly associated with comprehensibility are vocabulary difficulty and sentence length. . . . The strongest factor of the two is vocabulary difficulty. . . . (Chall, 1984, pp. 237-238)

Simple words are easiest to understand. Strunk and White (1979, p. 76) provide sage advice: "Do not be tempted by a twenty-dollar word when there is a ten-center handy, ready and able." *Utilize* is a good example of a twenty-dollar word. Follett (1966, p. 221) singles it out for criticism:

> It should seem as if . . . no word could be called needless. Exact synonyms are rare, and there is always a feature in the apparent synonym, whether shade of meaning, connotation, length, or rhythm, by which it can make itself useful. Yet some words at some times and others at all times can be shown to be unnecessary. *Utilize* is one of the second class. The occasions when *use* will not do are so rare as to be inexistant for the workaday writer, and the bad habit of resorting to the longer word becomes incurable.[1]

The Handbook of Technical Communication (Brusaw, Alred, & Oliu, 1987, p. 395) lists other long words and their preferred counterparts: *analyzitation* (prefer *analysis*), *certificated* (prefer *certified*), *commercialistic* (prefer *commercial*), *interconnect* (prefer *connect*), *finalize* (prefer *finish*), *orientate* (prefer *orient*), *prioritization* (prefer *priority*), and *visitation* (prefer *visit*).

The requirement to use short words should be applied with some common sense, however. Not all long words are uncommon and not all short words are common: "Multisyllable words like *butterfly*, *everyone*, *however*, and *neighborhood* are . . . familiar . . . , while short words like *adz*, *bleb*, *emir*, and *hadj* are not" (Stratton, 1984, p. 435). Further, common words, in this context, are words that procedure users commonly encounter. There is nothing wrong with using a long

---

[1]Strunk and White (1979, p. 63), who tend to be much more concise, provide similar, though greatly abbreviated guidance: "Utilize. Prefer use."

word if you are certain your users will understand it and there are no shorter alternatives available.

Some writers may be concerned that simple, common words cannot effectively communicate complex technical concepts. Yet, simple words can be used effectively with little loss in meaning, as indicated by recent efforts to develop a simplified English vocabulary set for some technical documents (Gringas, 1987). Although these efforts are intended mainly to facilitate the translation of documents into other languages, their success indicates that simple words can communicate effectively.

Finally, the illiteracy rates in this country provide an additional reason to use simpler words. It is estimated that approximately 19% of the workforce in the United States cannot read at the eighth-grade level and 30% of the workforce cannot read at the tenth-grade level (Washington State Office of Financial Management, 1990). Although it is likely that illiteracy rates are lower within the technological settings where procedures are used, as a procedure writer, you must deal with the unfortunate possibility that some of your users may have difficulty reading. The use of simpler, shorter words can make procedures more accessible to these individuals.

6.3   Avoid words that may be misunderstood.

Summary

Procedure writers should avoid words that may be misunderstood, either in written or spoken form. Substitute a clearer word or phrase for the ambiguous word.

Discussion

It would be impractical to require that words with multiple meanings not be used in procedures, as nearly every word in the English language has more than one meaning. These multiple meanings typically are not problematic. It is a normal part of the reading process to attach meanings to words based on context. When we read the sentence, *John will file the memo*, we know that *file* is a verb describing an action and not a noun describing a large metal cabinet, a set of data that can be read by a computer, or a tool for grating metal. We attach different meanings to *file* when we read *John put the memo in the file*, or *Lotus can't read my file*, or *The prisoner had a file baked in a cake*.

Problems are likely to arise, however, when the meaning of a word is not evident based on context. As a procedure writer, you must ensure that your instructions will be understood by avoiding ambiguous words. *Open the right valve* is unclear; *Open the right-hand valve* is preferable. *Recover* and *re-cover* (meaning to cover again) would also be confusing; instead of using *re-cover*, you should specifically request that users *cover the opening again*.

Problems may also arise when instructions in a procedure are given orally. Many words sound alike. You should avoid these words also. *Increase* and *decrease*, for example, can be confused with each other; *raise* and *reduce* are preferable.

Some words by their nature are abstract and vague, such as the adverb *slowly* in *He drove slowly*. Houp and Pearsall (1988, p. 147) acknowledge the need for such abstract words, but warn that writers must be cautious: "Abstractions are needed for generalizing, but they cannot replace specific words and necessary details. Words mean different things to different people. The higher you go on the abstraction ladder, the truer this is. Abstract words [can be] interpreted in as many different ways as the writer has readers." Slowly at the Indianapolis 500 is different than slowly in a school zone.

In procedures, vague words are most likely to be adverbs, which modify verbs, or adjectives, which modify nouns. If users are instructed to *Slowly drain the tank*, they must attach a specific rate to the adverb *slowly*. If they read the step *IF the mechanism is rusty, THEN replace it*, what constitutes *rusty* (an adjective)? Whenever possible, adverbs and adjectives should be quantified; say, *Drain the tank at a rate no greater than 10 gallons/minute* or *IF at least 15% of the mechanism's surface area is rusted, THEN replace it*. An illustration of the mechanism showing an acceptable level of rust might also be useful.

Sometimes you are forced to use a vague adverb or adjective. Returning to the example of the rusty mechanism, perhaps the 15% level doesn't work because the decision to replace the mechanism hinges on which part is rusted or the nature of the rust and the whole issue is simply too complicated to explain—but an experienced maintainer will know whether the mechanism should be replaced. In such a case, it is acceptable to include the adjective, but during validation and verification you should ensure that it will not be misunderstood.

6.4   Restrict the use of abbreviations and acronyms.

Summary

All abbreviations and acronyms used in procedures should be taken from a restricted list. Users should know the meaning of all abbreviations and acronyms used in procedures without referring to this list.

Discussion

Abbreviations are abridged word contractions, such as *fig* for figure, *govt* for government, or *op* for operations. Acronyms are representative words formed from letters (usually initials) of words in a defining phrase. Acronyms may be pronounced as words, such as NASA for National Aeronautics and Space Administration, or pronounced letter by letter, such as COD (i.e, *see-oh-dee*) for cash on delivery. In some reference manuals, both of these word-contracting methods are combined under the single heading of abbreviations, as the distinction between acronyms and abbreviations is slight (Towell, 1989). Both methods are used to increase reading speed and accuracy as well as conserve space on the page. For the sake of simplification, the following discussion will use *abbreviations* as an umbrella term for acronyms and abbreviations.

Used within certain limitations, abbreviations can assist the reader. Often, readers will be more familiar with the abbreviation than the term it represents. If a word or phrase is commonly understood and used throughout the procedure (e.g., *safety analysis report*), it is appropriate to use its abbreviated form (e.g., *SAR*), as this will conserve space on the page while increasing reading speed without jeopardizing comprehension. The shortened visual format of abbreviations, when understood by the reader, can be read faster than the word in full (because fewer letters can be scanned more quickly). In these situations, the use of abbreviations is acceptable and even preferable. However, abbreviations should *not* be used simply for the procedure writer's convenience. Don't include an abbreviation simply to avoid typing the complete word or phrase.

In some documents, it is acceptable to define an abbreviation the first time it appears. This is not an acceptable practice in procedures, however. Procedures are not always performed from start to finish; users may follow a cross-reference to the middle of a procedure and begin the procedure at that point or may only perform one section of a procedure. In these situations, the user may miss the initial definition of the abbreviation. Also, procedure readers have enough demands on them without being expected to learn the meanings of abbreviations as they are encountered. You should use only abbreviations that are familiar to the user and that users will understand without definition (Rogers & Moeller, 1984).

The best way to ensure that abbreviations will be understood is to use only abbreviations from an approved list. This list should be included in the writers' guide. Only in rare cases will it be necessary to deviate from the standardized list, in order to copy exact wording from inconsistent nameplates or equipment labels. In these cases, it is more important that the procedural text be representative of the actual equipment markings than that all abbreviations conform in the abbreviation list.

Several rules govern the abbreviations on this list:

- Users should know the meaning of all abbreviations on the list without referring to the list. User comprehension should be tested before the abbreviation is accepted for use.

- This list should not include abbreviations that have more than one meaning or may be easily confused with other words. Avoid truncating words to create abbreviations that could be confused with other words (e.g., *king* for *kingdom*, *man* for *management*).

- Avoid using abbreviations that end in a period, because users may believe that the period indicates the end of a sentence.

- An abbreviation should represent only one term. For example, HP should not stand for both *horsepower* and *health physics*. You should also be careful of abbreviations that can be confused with other meanings when made plural; for example OPs (for *operating procedures*) could be confused with OPS for *operations*.

- Similarly, do not use more than one abbreviation to represent a single term. For example, the word *manager* could be abbreviated as *mngr* or *mgr*. Using only one of these (say, *mgr*) will reduce the amount of information the reader has to remember, and it will be clear that *mgr* (and only *mgr*) will stand for *manager*. Another example would be if the name of a piece of equipment was abbreviated in two different ways, like travel lock being abbreviated TRVL LCK and TVL LK; only one of these should be used.[2]

- Simple words are easily recognized and understood, and should therefore be left unaltered. Abbreviating simple words will increase the potential for reader confusion while the only benefit is that an already-short word is shortened further.

Remember—the purpose of abbreviating is to increase reading speed and to aid comprehension. Minimize the use of abbreviations, and stick to the list of approved abbreviations when writing procedures.

---

[2]Problems can sometimes arise if abbreviations refer to equipment labels and those labels are inconsistent; for example, *travel lock* may be labeled TRVL LCK in one place and TVL LK in another. In this unfortunate situation, if the labeling cannot be corrected, it is more important that procedure conform to the equipment label, so the procedure writer may be forced into using inconsistent abbreviations.

Chapter 7

Punctuation

This chapter discusses punctuation. One principle is presented.

7.1 Use punctuation that conforms to standard American English usage whenever possible.

Summary

Punctuation in procedures should conform to standard English usage, as this use of punctuation will conform to users' expectations. Complex or unconventional punctuation should be avoided.

Discussion

A reader's interpretation of a written passage or set of instructions is equally based upon both the author's word choice and use of punctuation. Punctuation takes the place of natural pauses, emphasis, and the voice inflections of speech. Brusaw, Alred, and Oliu (1987, p. 537) say that "punctuation often substitutes for the writer's facial expressions." Waller (1982) feels strongly about the importance of proper punctuation. He explained that punctuation serves two roles: one towards the reader and one for the writer. Punctuation marks serve the reader by guiding him or her much as a band leader guides the musicians. For the writer, punctuation is part of his or her "expressive repertoire" (Waller, 1982, p. 138).

The Role and Importance of Punctuation

There is a tendency to simplify the use of punctuation (Bernstein, 1965). Too little punctuation is risky because of the possibility the reader may misunderstand important information. Too much punctuation may be equally confusing because the reader might not be able to find important information.

Because punctuation guides readers and aids them in interpreting sentences, it is very important that writers use punctuation marks consistently by following standardized rules. Punctuation began to be standardized about the middle of the 19th century. As the industrial revolution generated the need for technical writing, it became necessary that readers and writers have an established common ground of understanding. This need is no less important today. Some writers misuse punctuation, using too little or too much, and claim author's license or style. This is acceptable for the poet or novelist; but the procedure writer must deliver a message or list of instructions in the simplest, most concise manner possible without drama, stylistic embellishment, or flowery prose. This necessity dictates the need for standardized punctuation.

Some Common Errors

It is not the intention or within the scope of this document to include an entire manual of punctuation in technical writing. There are many authoritative volumes on this subject readily available such as *Words into Type* (1974) and *The Chicago Manual of Style* (1982). An overview of selected punctuation standards and usage, however, may be beneficial.

You should select a word order that minimizes the need for punctuation. Break sentences that require extensive punctuation into shorter sentences. Excessive use of punctuation may be an indication that the information is too complex or that the writer is not organized and is perhaps even confused about the subject matter. The procedure writer must appear knowledgeable if a user is to give the written material credibility.

Shaw (1963, p. 5) presents a fun example of the importance of punctuation: *Jones where Smith had had had had had had had had had had had the examiners' approval.* Without changing word order and by making two sentences, this unintelligible jumble can be made to make reasonable sense. Using punctuation correctly, thereby directing the reader to pause appropriately, the phrase becomes understandable as follows: *Jones, where Smith had had "had had," had had "had." "Had had" had had the examiners' approval.*

Another example equally illustrates the importance of proper punctuation: *That that is is that that is not is not is that it it is.* Again, this phrase becomes meaningful as follows: *That that is, is. That that is not, is not. Is that it? It is.* Of course, these two examples are unusual and are used only as demonstrations of how important proper punctuation can be. But punctuation is critical to meaning.

Commas guide our interpretation of modifying clauses. For example, in the sentence *The annual report, which was distributed on Tuesday, shows that sales increased 25 percent last year* the commas surrounding the clause *which was distributed on Tuesday* tell the reader that he or she has come upon a nonrestrictive clause in the sentence. Given the commas around the clause, the reader knows that he or she could omit the information between the commas from the sentence without changing the meaning of the sentence. In other words, it is nice but not imperative for the reader to know that the annual report was distributed on Tuesday. If the commas were omitted from the sentence, however, and the *which* were changed to *that*, the clause *that was distributed Tuesday* could not be left out of the sentence without changing the sentence's meaning. Without the commas surrounding the clause, the sentence means that a particular annual report (the one distributed on Tuesday as opposed to the one distributed on Friday, perhaps) cited a 25 percent sales increase. The presence and position of the commas in the sentence guides the reader in interpreting what information is important for the meaning of the sentence as well as what information is supplemental to the meaning of the sentence.

Commas are also essential for clarifying lists. The comma before the *and* in a list can be particularly problematic. In technical writing, including procedures, it is recommended that a comma always be placed before the *and* (or *or*) in a list (e.g., *Blue, red, and green are my favorite colors*). If this rule is adhered to rigorously, confusion can be eliminated. Consider the sentence, *Frank, Bill and Jane completed the manuscript.* Is Frank being told that Bill and Jane completed the manuscript or did the three of them complete the manuscript? With the comma before the *and*, the sentence becomes unambiguous: *Frank, Bill, and Jane completed the manuscript.* All three of them worked on the manuscript.

Refer to one of the many books on punctuation for more detailed information on comma usage. Here are several reminders when using commas that may be helpful in procedure writing: use a comma to (1) separate clauses in technical statements; (2) separate procedure numbers, titles, and step numbers in cross-references; (3) separate appendix numbers and titles in references to appendices; and (4) clarify numbers of four or more digits.

We all know a period indicates the end of a declarative sentence and is considered a major pause. Periods also have other uses such as at the end of some, but not all, abbreviations. It is best to avoid periods at the end of acronyms or non-standard abbreviations. Standard abbreviations are those that are used often, such as Mr., Ms., and Dr. Certain specialized abbreviations such as SESS, AFAS, and SIAS do not require periods because a reader might interpret a period at the end of an abbreviation as meaning the end of a sentence. This could be confusing. (Section 6.4 discusses abbreviations in more detail.)

Other uses for a period in procedure writing are (1) at the end of an action step, (2) as a decimal point, (3) between a figure number and title in the title of the figure, and (4) between a table number and title in the title of the table.

There may be a temptation to use two periods when a sentence ends with an abbreviation, such as *The book was published by Jones Press, Inc..* The second period should not be used. The correct punctuation of this sentence is *The book was published by Jones Press, Inc.*

Procedure writers often use the colon (:). The most important use of the colon is to indicate that a list is to follow. The colon indicates to the reader that the following list belongs with the sentence.

The apostrophe (') is both a punctuation mark and a symbol for an omitted letter. George Bernard Shaw and others felt that using an apostrophe to replace perfectly good letters was lazy and without merit (Shaw, 1963). The procedure writer certainly does not want to appear interested in taking the easiest route for its own sake and should avoid using the apostrophe as a contraction. For example, _IF the pump is running_ is preferable to _IF the pump's running_.

The apostrophe does have a place in procedures, however. It shows possession and therefore indicates who or what is doing an action. When showing possession with a word ending in an _s_ or _s_-sound, the apostrophe should be placed at the end of the word. Examples of this are words such as _Jones_ and _kings_, where it is acceptable to write _Jones's_ or _kings's_ but more professional and attractive to write _Jones'_ or _kings'_. The meaning is the same and a reader should have no trouble understanding your intent.

Plural acronyms may also call for an apostrophe but, at least in technical writing, this is a standard that is beginning to lessen. It is acceptable to some authorities to write _COD's_ to show more than one COD. A suggested alternative is to write _CODs_, however, as the type will appear cleaner and more attractive while eliminating any possibility that you mean to indicate possession (something belonging to more than a COD).

In some instances, however, the punctuation used in procedures should differ from standard practice. For example, in many types of writing, it is a common custom to hyphenate words at syllable breaks at the end of a line. In right-justified text, hyphenation allows greater control over the spaces between the words in a line, and can improve the appearance of the text. This advantage does not pertain to text that is ragged right, as is the text in procedures (see Section 11.3). In procedures, hyphenation serves only to fit more words onto the line. The cost is that the procedure is more difficult to read, as a single word is split between two lines (Hartley, 1982). Hyphenation should be avoided in procedures.

Chapter 8

Level of Detail

As a procedure writer, one of the most difficult aspects of your job will be to write procedures at the appropriate level of detail—procedures should contain neither too little nor too much information. This chapter discusses this challenge. It presents one principle.

8.1 Write procedures at a level of detail that is appropriate for the procedures' intended users.

Summary

Procedures should be written at an appropriate level of detail, presenting neither too little nor too much information. The appropriate level of detail will vary according to the type of procedure, the frequency with which the procedure is performed, and the experience level of the users. Procedure writers should solicit feedback from users and interact with training personnel during procedure development, as both these activities are important for ensuring that the level of detail is correct.

Discussion

Level of detail refers to the match between the information provided in the procedure and the users' knowledge and ability. The procedure should not provide too little information, nor should it be cluttered with excessive detail.

It would be impossible to write a procedure for a completely ignorant audience. At a minimum, you must assume a working knowledge of the English language. In any kind of procedure, you must assume much more; in fact, you may be surprised to realize how much you do assume when writing procedures. Consider Figure 8.1, which presents steps from a laboratory procedure.

[1]	Add the following to 1 liter of deionized H_2O in a 2 liter beaker:

  •   1 ml Strontium, 20 mg/ml, carrier
       solution   ___

  •   1 ml Barium, 10 mg/ml, carrier
       solution   ___

  •   5 ml Calcium, 2M carrier solution   ___

[2]   IF the sample has been acidified,
           THEN neutralize it with 6N NaOH using
           a pH meter.   ___

[3]   Stir and heat to near boiling on a hot plate.   ___

[4]   Add 30 ml 3N Na_2CO_3 with stirring.   ___

[5]   Add 1-2 ml 6N NaOH and continue heating for one more
           minute.   ___

[6]   Remove from the hot plate and cool in a water bath.   ___

[7]   Decant the supernate and transfer the precipitate to
           a 250 ml centrifuge bottle.   ___

[8]   Centrifuge the solution and discard the supernate.   ___

Figure 8.1. Excerpt from a Chemistry Procedure. This procedure assumes a high level of laboratory expertise on the part of its users.

Clearly, the users of this procedure must be well versed in laboratory practices and techniques; otherwise, they will be unable to execute the procedure. They must understand terms such as *supernate* and *precipitate*, they must know how to prepare the required solutions, they must know how to operate a centrifuge, and so forth. If the procedure user has these skills, then a procedure written in this manner is not only acceptable, it is preferable, because the user does not have to wade through unnecessary information.

The determination of the correct level of detail is a difficult, important task that has a greater effect on procedure comprehensibility than does syntax or sentence structure. Bovair and Kieras (1989, p. 18) discuss a study that evaluated different versions of written instructions where

> the good and bad instructions could not be distinguished by text characteristics likely to affect reading comprehension such as length of text or length of sentences; indeed, some of the best instructions had the most complex syntax and sentence structure. The most important differences between good and bad instructions seemed to be those of content; in particular, poor instructions omitted important details like the orientation of parts in the assembly task, and often included the wrong level of detail.

While these findings certainly are not justifications to ignore step syntax and structure, they clearly point out the importance of level of detail in procedures.

The Dangers of Too Little or Too Much Detail

A procedure can present detail at a variety of levels. Figure 8.2 provides examples of various levels of detail.

Few would argue that procedures that include inadequate detail can lead to error. Obviously, a procedure cannot assist users in executing tasks if the procedure is incomplete *from the user's point of view*. A given level of detail is appropriate relative to the user's knowledge and experience. Berry (1981) warns that procedure writers should not assume knowledge that the user may not have and that procedure writers who may be intimately familiar with the procedure or the system being documented may leave out information that is important for the novice user. A recent study examining the occurrence of procedure violations in U.S. nuclear power plants points out the consequences that too little detail in procedures can have for safety in nuclear facilities. Barnes et al. (in press) found that an inadequate level of detail in procedures was the most frequently cited cause of procedure-related errors in licensee event reports between January of 1984 and July of 1988.[1]

However, it can be just as bad to include too much information in the procedure. Huckin (1983, p. 98) states,

> Research by information theorists suggests that the use of extended analogies, elaborate examples, and other lengthy explications of important concepts may do more harm than good, if the concepts being explained are already familiar to the reader and can be succinctly related to already-familiar concepts. . . . Explications

---

[1]Licensee event reports are self-reports of abnormal or unusual occurrences that commercial nuclear power plants file with the Nuclear Regulatory Commission.

that are unnecessarily long raise the proportion of redundant
information and risk boring the reader to the point of inattention.

While procedures are unlikely to include the "extended analogies, elaborate
examples, and other lengthy explications of important concepts" of which Huckin
writes, these findings point out the danger of including excessive information of
any type in the procedure. As procedure writers may feel the urge to "play it
safe" and include excessive detail, the problem of a level of detail that is too high
can be likely.

[1]	Isolate letdown line.	—
[1]	Isolate letdown line by closing CV1214 and CV1216.	—
[1]	Isolate the letdown line by closing valves CV1214 and CV1216. Controls are on panel C18.	—
[1]	Isolate the letdown line by first closing valve CV1214 and then by closing valve CV1218. Controls are on panel C18. Indicator lights are on panels C15 and C16.	—
[1]	Go to panel C18.	—
[2]	Close valve CV1214 by turning the knob to the right until full stop.	—
[3]	Go to panel C16.	—
[4]	Check that the lamp indicator for CV1214 is green.	—
[5]	Go to panel C18.	—
[6]	Close valve CV1216 by turning the knob to the right until full stop.	—
[7]	Go to panel C15.	—
[8]	Check that the lamp indicator for CV1216 is green.	—

Figure 8.2. Various Levels of Detail. An identical step is presented at varying levels of
detail. (Adapted from Zach, 1980)

All procedures assume a certain base level of knowledge on the part of users. For instance, an emergency operating procedure requires that operators trip the reactor without explaining how to do so; a maintenance procedure requires that users loosen a bolt without explaining which way to turn it; administrative procedures contain requirements for subordinates to communicate with managers without discussing office protocol. If procedures did not make this assumption, they would be impossible to use; remember that too much detail can make the procedure as confusing as too little. As an exercise, you might try to write a procedure for some common task, say leaving the house in the morning. Include *every* detail you can think of. Is the procedure usable?

In the context of emergency operating procedures in commercial reactors, Fuchs, Engelschall, and Imlay (1981, p. 2-13) address the problem of excessive detail:

> In several of the procedures evaluated, extraneous explanatory information is included. . . . Sometimes this information is included in steps; at other times it takes the form of excessive cautions and notes. Citing this as a deficiency is not intended to question the value of such information. Explanatory information serves to motivate the operator and, most importantly, help him understand what is happening. However, such information belongs in training, not in an emergency procedure. In an emergency, the operator needs to know *what to do and how to do it*. If he's faced with an unforeseen situation, it is too late for him to learn how the system works and why certain actions must be taken. Such information should be carried by system explanation manuals to be used in the operator training program.

It is important to realize, however, that the appropriate level of detail in an emergency operating procedure is different from the appropriate level of detail in other types of procedures. Procedures that are seldom performed, are not covered extensively (or at all) in user training, or are not executed under time constraints may have a higher level of detail than emergency operating procedures, which typically present information most concisely.

Audience Analysis

It is difficult in a book such as this, which applies to a range of different procedures used in a range of facilities, to provide specific information on level of detail. Instead, the purpose here is to provide you with the technique that you will use in determining the appropriate level of detail in a particular situation. The primary technique that you will use is *audience analysis*.

Audience analysis is the skill (or art) of studying your audience (procedure users) so that you can prepare a document that they will understand and can use. *The Handbook of Technical Writing* explains the importance of audience analysis:

> The first rule of effective writing is to help the reader. The responsibility that technical writers have to their readers is nicely expressed in the Society of Technical Communication's *Code for Communicators*, which calls for technical writers to hold themselves responsible for how well their audience understands their message and to satisfy the readers' need for information rather than the writer's need for self expression. This code reminds writers to concentrate on writing *for* the needs of specific readers rather than merely *about* certain subjects. (Brusaw, Alred, & Oliu, 1987, p. 550)

Issues of audience analysis in procedures are concerned primarily with determining the appropriate level of detail. In other types of writing, such as reports, articles, or business letters, technical communicators must also consider issues of style and tone. For example, a writer preparing a memo to the president of a large company must be concerned that the memo is written in a relatively formal style and has a respectful tone (assuming that the president prefers that type of relationship with his or her subordinates). The format and content of procedures are so constrained, however, that these issues largely become moot, and audience analysis reduces primarily to determining the appropriate level of detail—which can still be quite a job.

To a certain extent, we perform a basic audience analysis without even thinking about it. In *Technical Writing: Process and Product*, Stratton (1984, p. 27) says,

> You will always have some notion of audience and purpose when you write; you will run into trouble only when your notions are too limited or when they fail to line up with those of the people who review and approve your writing. It behooves you, then, as a communicator of technical information to take some specific steps to determine audience, purpose, and other design criteria for each of your communication contexts and to document your analysis.

Basically, you want to stay in touch with the users of the procedures—*don't write in isolation*. As a procedure writer, you are very fortunate because you can meet and talk with the readers of your documents; few other technical communicators have this luxury. They must guess at their audience's characteristics or analyze a small sample of their audience and hope that this analysis will generalize to the audience as a whole. You should take advantage of this opportunity and work at maintaining open lines of communication between yourself and your users.

This communication can be formal or informal. During validation and verification, you will receive formal feedback. It is up to you to generate sources of informal feedback. Cultivate relationships with users whose input you value. Bounce ideas off them, especially if you are experiencing writer's block. Pass drafts of your procedures around to your colleagues for review and discuss common problems that you are having.

The feedback that will result from these open lines of communication can be difficult to take; most people dislike their writing criticized. You should try to separate your ego from your writing and realize that users have a different perspective that will complement and contribute to your writing. No one writes so well that his or her writing cannot be improved by an intelligent, constructive evaluation.

The Relationship Between Level of Detail and Training

The passage from Fuchs, Engelschall, and Imlay quoted earlier in this section said that some information should be covered in training rather than included in procedures. In facilities with formal training on procedures, training has a large effect on the user's knowledge level. Consequently, it is important that procedure writers work with trainers (and visa versa).

There are definite advantages to coordinating procedure writing and training. An important advantage is the coordination of level of detail. Training personnel can tell procedure writers that a procedure assumes knowledge that is not covered in the training program or that a procedure unnecessarily includes information that is well covered in training. When such discrepancies arise, they can be addressed either by modifying the procedure or the training curriculum, whichever is more appropriate. Also, if procedure writers and trainers work together, then trainers may be able to use the procedures more effectively during training sessions. Coordination between procedure writing and training is a prerequisite to effective procedures.

Presenting Varying Levels of Detail with the Actions-Details Format

Thus far, this section has discussed level of detail as though one level of detail is suitable for all users. Common sense should tell you that this is not the case. Users are different and require various levels of detail. Such differences in abilities should not be taken as a criticism of users; indeed, a user who may be unfamiliar with one procedure may be intimately familiar with other procedures. It is merely an acknowledgement that people can be different.

The procedure should address the needs of the least-skilled user. However, if there is a large gap between the skill levels of the most- and least-skilled users, then the procedure writer is confronted with a problem that will be difficult to address effectively with a procedure. Instead, the problem should be rectified through changes in training, work assignments, or the like.

There are, however, ways to write procedures so that they effectively and simultaneously present information at various levels of detail. The ideal solution would be an on-line procedure that would tailor itself according to the needs of the user. Although the technology for developing on-line procedures clearly exists, it has yet to be widely adopted. Also, on-line procedures are not appropriate for all tasks and environments.

But all is not lost. The actions-details format, where the left column presents actions and the right column presents details, can be surprisingly effective for addressing the needs of both experienced and inexperienced users. Figure 8.3 shows an example of the actions-details format.

The advantage of the actions-details format is that actions and details are clearly differentiated, allowing users who do not need the information in the details column to easily bypass that information. If the information in the details column were included in a single column, as shown in Figure 8.4, the resulting steps would appear wordy and difficult to read. The actions-details format allows identical information to be presented in a much cleaner fashion.

The actions-details format is particularly well suited to facilities with a verbatim compliance policy of procedure execution. A verbatim compliance policy requires that procedures be executed exactly as they are written. The advantage of a verbatim compliance policy is that it allows management greater control over work processes. The disadvantages are that the procedure *must* be correct, or else the procedure user is put in the bind of being required to follow an inaccurate procedure. Some procedure users may also see a verbatim compliance policy as an affront to their skill and experience. The actions-details format allows a verbatim compliance policy to be implemented in a more flexible fashion. If verbatim compliance can be required only for the actions column, users may follow the details column if they wish, but are free to deviate from it as long as they accomplish the instructions included in the actions column.

The actions-details format is presented here as one way of addressing the level-of-detail problem. While effective procedures can be written in the single-column format, facilities confronting level-of-detail problems in their procedures may wish to consider the actions-details format.

<u>Actions</u>	<u>Details</u>
___ **[7]** Turn on the turbine generator core monitor.	Depress the POWER pushbutton on panel GHN-AR-26, which is located on the Turbine Generator Recorder Cabinet, ZJN-C07, behind the control room.
___ **[8]** Record the time the core monitor was turned on in the control room logs.	
___ **[9]** Start Motor Suction Pump, LON-P03.	Take MOTOR SUCTION PUMP P03, LON-HS-21, to the START position and check that the red indicator light comes on.
___**[10]** Direct a nuclear operator to check that the Main Shaft Oil Pump Suction Pressure Indicator, LON-PI-70, reads between 15 and 25 psig.	LON-PI-70 is located on the main turbine front standard.
___**[11]** Direct a nuclear operator to transfer and maintain temperature control of the main turbine to manual.	Directions for local operations are provided for the nuclear operator in Appendix Y.
___ **[12]** Check that turbine bearing oil temperatures are between 130 and 150°F.	Use temperature recorder MTNTR-303, Points 1 through 12, on board B07.
___ **[13]** IF the AUTO ACTUATE OUT OF SERVICE LIGHT is <u>NOT</u> on, <u>THEN</u> PERFORM Section 8.0 of Reactor Power Cutback, 41OP-1SF04. RETURN TO Step **[14]** in this procedure.	The AUTO ACTUATE OUT OF SERVICE light is located on the REACTOR POWER CUTBACK panel on board B04.

Figure 8.3. Actions-Details Format. In the actions-details format, the left column presents actions while the right column presents detailed information on the performance of those actions. Users who are familiar with the procedure need only look at the actions column; users who need more information can refer to the details column as necessary. The procedure effectively presents two levels of detail.

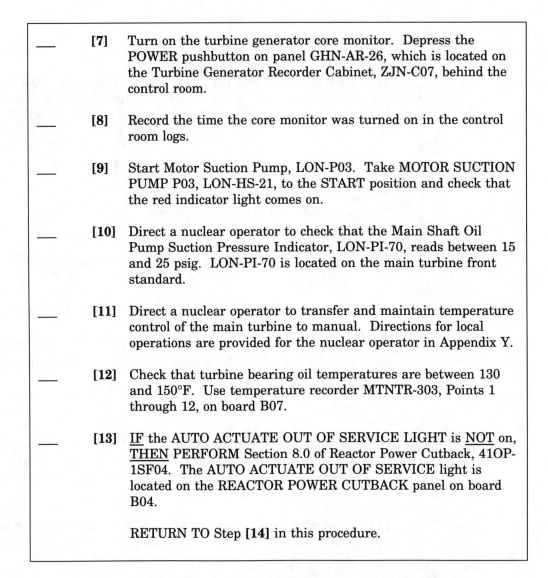

___ [7]   Turn on the turbine generator core monitor. Depress the
           POWER pushbutton on panel GHN-AR-26, which is located on
           the Turbine Generator Recorder Cabinet, ZJN-C07, behind the
           control room.

___ [8]   Record the time the core monitor was turned on in the control
           room logs.

___ [9]   Start Motor Suction Pump, LON-P03. Take MOTOR SUCTION
           PUMP P03, LON-HS-21, to the START position and check that
           the red indicator light comes on.

___ [10] Direct a nuclear operator to check that the Main Shaft Oil
           Pump Suction Pressure Indicator, LON-PI-70, reads between 15
           and 25 psig. LON-PI-70 is located on the main turbine front
           standard.

___ [11] Direct a nuclear operator to transfer and maintain temperature
           control of the main turbine to manual. Directions for local
           operations are provided for the nuclear operator in Appendix Y.

___ [12] Check that turbine bearing oil temperatures are between 130
           and 150°F. Use temperature recorder MTNTR-303, Points 1
           through 12, on board B07.

___ [13] IF the AUTO ACTUATE OUT OF SERVICE LIGHT is NOT on,
           THEN PERFORM Section 8.0 of Reactor Power Cutback, 41OP-
           1SF04. The AUTO ACTUATE OUT OF SERVICE light is
           located on the REACTOR POWER CUTBACK panel on board
           B04.

           RETURN TO Step [14] in this procedure.

Figure 8.4. Excessive Detail Presented in the Single-Column Format. These steps,
which are identical in content to those in Figure 8.3, are wordy and difficult to follow when
presented in the single-column format.

Chapter 9

Numerical Information

Numerical information is any information associated with numbers presented in a procedure. Numerical information can include readings from instrument displays, calculated values, or control settings. Five principles regarding the use of numbers in procedures are presented in this chapter:

- Differentiate between the use of Arabic and spelled-out numbers in a consistent, useful fashion.

- Include units of measure with numerical information whenever appropriate.

- Do not specify numbers at a greater precision than can be read from instrument panel displays.

- Specify ranges rather than error bands.

- Avoid requiring users to make calculations in procedures; if a calculation is required, use a calculation aid.

9.1 Differentiate between the use of Arabic and spelled-out numbers in a consistent, useful fashion.

Summary

As a general rule, procedures should use Arabic numbers (e.g., 0, 1, 2, 3) rather than spelled-out numbers or Roman numerals.

Discussion

Of all of the issues facing writers, the presentation of numerical information is one of the simplest yet most troublesome. The important point is to develop a rule that addresses the few basic issues discussed in this section and to apply that rule consistently. The guidance provided in *Words Into Type* (1974, p. 125) is sound: "In scientific and technical writing the rule is to use numerals for all physical measures and for most quantities of 11 and over." Some facilities may prefer to use numerals entirely; this guidance is also sound, provided that spelled-out numerals are used in the few instances where the use of numerals could be confusing.

In most cases, numbers in procedures will refer to physical quantities (i.e., are accompanied by a unit of measure) and are most concisely presented in numerals. Hence, *90 dB(A)*, *5 seconds*, *1200 rpm*, *4.16 kV*, and *2%* are all acceptable. If a number is not accompanied by a unit of measure and is 11 or greater, numerals should again be used. If a number is not accompanied by a unit of measure and is less than 11, it may be spelled out or presented in numerals, depending on the specifications in the writers' guide; in other words, *Start 1 reactor coolant pump* is acceptable, as is *Start one reactor coolant pump*. It is important, however, that a consistent approach be adopted.

Yet, in two instances, a spelled-out number is preferable for preventing confusion. The first of these occurs when a number without a unit of measure is followed directly by a number that is accompanied by a unit of measure, as in *Energize one 4.16 kV bus*. In this case, the first number should be spelled out; if the step read *Energize 1 4.16 kV bus*, users might misread it as a 14.16 kV bus.

The second instance occurs when a number (particularly a single-digit number) is emphasized. Compare the examples in Figure 9.1.

Use <u>1</u> of the following:	Use <u>one</u> of the following:
Use **1** of the following:	Use **one** of the following:
Use *1* of the following:	Use *one* of the following:

Figure 9.1. Emphasis of Numerals. Because single-digit numerals are physically so small, the spelled-out version of the number is more effectively emphasized when typographic emphasis techniques are used.

Figure 9.1 shows how typographic emphasis techniques (discussed in Chapter 13) are more effective on spelled-out numbers because they are physically larger than their numerical equivalents. Thus, numbers that (1) are emphasized and (2) are not accompanied by a unit of measure should be spelled out.

9.2   Include units of measure with numerical information whenever appropriate.

Summary

Units of measure should always be used to avoid ambiguity. Units of measure must match the panel or instrument markings exactly.

Discussion

Units of measure provide important information. Units of measure specify exactly what a number represents. For example, 60 miles per hour (miles/hour) specifies exactly what is being discussed, where as 60 can be 60 of anything. Units of measure should always be included to avoid ambiguity and to assist the user in correctly performing the required action. It is a mistake to assume that the units of measure will be obvious to the user.

A critical aspect of providing units of measure in numerical information is that the units of measure must match the panel or instrument markings exactly (NRC, 1982). For example, if a temperature gauge is marked in degrees Fahrenheit (°F), then any temperatures related to this gauge must be given in degrees Fahrenheit, as in 175°F. If the unit of measure is left off (175°), then there is ambiguity in whether Fahrenheit or Celsius is used. Another example is in the use of English or metric measurement. Gasoline may be dispensed in gallons or liters. If there is no marking on the pump, or in any directions, then it is difficult to know which is being used. Units of measure for pressure can also be problematic. Sometimes psi (pounds per square inch) is not a sufficient unit and a more specific unit of measure, such as psia (psi atmosphere) or psig (psi gauge), must be used. Users should not be required to convert seconds into minutes if seconds are the unit of measure used on a chronometer.

9.3   Do not specify numbers at a greater precision than can be read from instrument panel displays.

Summary

In presenting numerical information in procedures, it is important to specify numbers only to the precision available on the instrument panel or display, because users cannot read the panels to a greater precision.

Discussion

Precision refers to the exactness with which a quantity is expressed. For example, a person might express his height as being about 6 feet, or more precisely, 5 feet 11 inches. This person might be even more precise and say that he is 5 feet 11-1/2 inches tall. Or, with very accurate measuring equipment, he may say that he is 5 feet 11.29456 inches tall. All these expressions of height represent different levels of precision.

In presenting numerical information in procedures, it is important to specify numbers only to the precision available on the instrument panel or display (or whatever the source of the numbers). For example, if an instrument displays only elapsed minutes, then the procedure should not ask for information about elapsed minutes *and* seconds. If an instrument dial can only be read to the nearest 5 (e.g., 95, 100, 105), then the procedure should not required the user to read 97. By presenting numerical information only to the precision that is available, you help the user read the numbers and not make mistakes or waste time trying to guess at numbers that cannot be easily read.

It is also wise to be conservative in the presentation of numerical information depending on the precision available on the instrumentation. If a technical specification calls for a value to be less than 2.57 units, and the instrumentation can only be read to the nearest 0.1 unit, then it is better to be conservative and use the value *less than 2.5 units*, rather than *2.6 units*. Using *2.6 units* could allow the value to exceed the technical specification.

9.4   Specify ranges rather than error bands.

Summary

Use ranges to specify acceptable limits. Explicit statements of the acceptable limits for particular values are easier to understand and reduce the chance of error. Error bands should not be used to express a range of values, as they require a mental calculation by the user. The user can make a mistake in adding or subtracting or can remember the numbers incorrectly.

Discussion

Sometimes a range of values, rather than a single value, is acceptable for a given parameter. When we speak of a range, we are talking about the extent or limits of acceptable values. There are several ways to express a group of acceptable values. One way is to specify a range, which gives the limits or outer boundaries of acceptable values. For example, 10-20 is a range. Another way to express acceptable values is by using error bands. Error bands show the acceptable deviation from a given number (e.g., 15±5).

Error bands require users to make a mental calculation. In the above example, the user must take the acceptable value and subtract 5 (to get 10) and add 5 (to get 20) and then hold that range of values (10-20) in memory while he or she checks the instrumentation to see if it corresponds to the acceptable range. Because error bands require a mental calculation, users are more prone to error. The user can make a mistake in adding or subtracting or can remember the numbers incorrectly. Therefore, error bands should not be used to express a range of values.

Instead, use ranges to specify acceptable limits. Explicitly stating the acceptable limits of the values reduces the opportunity for error. By presenting a range (e.g., 10-20), mental calculations are avoided and the burden on the memory is reduced. The values are written and available to check. Optimal or normal values can still be specified, but include the acceptable range rather than an error band. For example, a normal value of 15 with an acceptable range of 10-20, can be expressed as *15 (range 10-20)* or *10-20 (normal 15)*. However, you should avoid cluttering the procedure with optimal values unless they are necessary.

Figure 9.2 rates the various formats for presenting acceptance values.

Good: IF the temperature is 75-85°F,
       THEN open the access door.

Bad: IF the temperature is 80°F (±5°F),
       THEN open the access door.

Ugly: IF the temperature is 80°F (±6.3%),
       THEN open the access door.

Figure 9.2. Presentation of Ranges. Ranges (the good example) are preferable to error bands (the bad example). The ugly example shows an example where the user must make a complex calculation, increasing the potential for error and slowing procedure execution.

9.5   Avoid requiring users to make calculations in procedures; if a calculation is required, use a calculation aid.

Summary

Calculations should be avoided whenever possible. There may be times when a calculation must be made. If so, provide a calculation aid. The use of calculation aids increases accuracy, leaves a record of data entries and computations, and facilitates traceability and verification.

Discussion

Calculations require some kind of numerical computing or manipulating. Calculations create opportunities for error. Calculations also require time. It is therefore recommended that calculations be avoided whenever possible. This guidance applies to simple calculations, such as adding error bands to the single value given (e.g., 2.5±0.1), as well as to long and complex calculations.

However, there may be times when a calculation must be made. If so, providing a calculation aid can minimize the problems discussed above. A calculation aid is anything that assists the user in performing the required calculation. Calculation aids should be clear, logically formatted and include necessary spaces for all data entries (NRC, 1982). Examples of calculation aids include (1) writing the required formula with blank spaces to insert the appropriate values or (2) using worksheets that describe the needed calculations.

By dictating the calculations to be performed (and their order) and by forcing users to record intermediate steps in a problem solution, a well-designed calculation aid can capture many of the most important strengths of graphic aids for problem solving (Larkin & Simon, 1987). Calculation aids spell out the calculation requirements, including units of measure and conversion factors. Aids are used to minimize memory requirements. Users do not have to remember the formula or how to do the calculation.

Calculation aids also provide a way to check the calculation easily. Because all the information is written down and does not need to be remembered, others can verify the accuracy of the calculation. Thus, the use of calculation aids increases accuracy, leaves a record of data entries and computations, and facilitates traceability and verification.

Figure 9.3 provides an example of a calculation aid.

[5]   Ensure that the total fissile g content of a waste
        package placed in any single soil vault is
        less than 300 g.

        [5.1]   Record current vault $_{235}$U g content   ___ g

        [5.2]   Record shipment $_{235}$U g content   ___ g

        [5.3]   Record subtotal (sum of [5.1] + [5.2])   ___ g

        [5.4]   Record current vault fissile g content
                  other than $_{235}$U and multiply by 2

                                                    _____ x 2 = ___ g

        [5.5]   Record shipment fissile g content
                  other than $_{235}$U and multiply by 2

                                                    _____ x 2 = ___ g

        [5.6]   Record subtotal (sum of [5.4] + [5.5])   ___ g

        [5.7]   Record total fissile g content
                  (sum of [5.3] + [5.6])   ___ g

[6]   IF total fissile g content is greater than 300 g,
        THEN immediately notify the Shift Manager.

Figure 9.3. Example of a Calculation Aid Included in a Procedure. This calculation aid
assists users in determining the weight of a shipment.

Part Three:
Format and Organization

Chapter 10

Introduction: Format and Organization

Many factors affect format, such as type font, indentation, emphasis techniques, and so on. Some documents, such as novels, have a very simple format. They consist of a series of paragraphs, one after another, so each page looks very much like the previous page. Other documents, such as procedures, have a more complex format. In procedures, the format provides useful information to users—indentation differentiates steps from substeps, emphasis techniques indicate the relative importance of items, and so on.

Part Three of this handbook discusses procedure format and organization. Format refers to the way a procedure looks. Organization refers to the order that information is presented and how that information is structured. Organization entails two things: (1) logical relationships in information (e.g., steps are grouped into sections) and (2) the sequence in which items are performed.

Part Three is divided into four chapters (besides this chapter):

- Chapter 11 discusses step format, including type size and font, white space (i.e., the blank space on the page), margins, and step numbering.

- Chapter 12 discusses placekeeping aids.

- Chapter 13 discusses emphasis techniques.

- Chapter 14 discusses procedure organization.

Chapter 11

Step Format

This chapter discusses step format, or the way steps should look. Three principles are presented:

- Use type that is readable in the worst conditions of expected use.

- Use white space according to the conventions of graphic design.

- Use ragged-right margins.

11.1 Use type that is readable in the worst conditions of expected use.

Summary

The readability of type is affected by its size, font, and case:

- A variety of factors complicate the readability of a type size. Because of these factors, this book does not specify a particular type size for procedures. Twelve-point type should be used as a starting point, with the realization that the optimal type size may differ depending on the situation.

- The choice of a type font is best based on a decision regarding which font appears to be the most readable under expected conditions of use.

- Blocks of text should appear in mixed case; all capitals should not be used as an emphasis technique for blocks of text (e.g., in cautions). However, individual words or phrases may be emphasized by the use of all capitals.

Discussion

This section discusses type size, type font, and type case in more detail:

- *Type size*, which is still defined based on the conventions used by printers who worked with mechanical printing presses, is the height of the block of lead in which a letter would be cast. This size is typically greater than the height of the letter.

- A *font* is the complete assortment of letters and characters of a single design, such as Times or Helvetica. *Typeface* is a synonym for *font*.

- *Case* refers to whether letters are uppercase (i.e., capital), lowercase, or some combination.

Type Size

The readability of type is greatly affected by its size; obviously, if type is too small, it cannot be read easily. The determination of adequate type size is as much an art as a science. Three considerations enter into an effective determination of type size:

- A visual angle formula can be used to calculate whether type is of sufficient size to be distinguished by the human eye, given a certain reading distance.

- Type size can be based on the length of a line of type.

- Type size can be determined subjectively.

This section will begin with a discussion of the visual angle formula, which is presented as a sort of a "straw man." Although the visual angle formula does have its uses, it should be supplemented with other information. Explaining why the visual angle formula falls short makes an important point about trying to characterize type size, or any other aspect of a procedure, in a mathematical formula.

The visual angle formula is a calculation that can be performed to ensure that a letter is sufficiently large for the eye to discern it. Obviously, the farther a letter is from the eye, the larger the letter must be. A convenient method for considering distance and type size together is to specify the visual angle that must be subtended by the letter. Figure 11.1 depicts the visual angle.

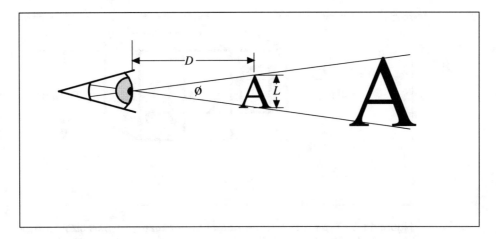

Figure 11.1. Visual Angle. The visual angle ($\varnothing$) is the angle subtended at the eye by the letter. Visual angle is used to conveniently take the size of a letter and its viewing distance into account. A single visual angle specifies a size for a letter at all viewing distances.

The following formula expresses the relationship between letter size (L), viewing distance (D), and visual angle ($\varnothing$). The visual angle is specified in degrees; L and D must be specified in identical units (e.g., inches).

$$\tan \frac{1}{2}\phi = 0.5\ \frac{L}{D}$$

Current design standards recommend that the visual angle be 0.172° for letters to be discernable to 90% by the population and 0.401° for letters to be discernable by "virtually 100%" of the population (Smith, 1979, p. 661). By setting $\varnothing$ equal to these values and solving for L, equations specifying L as a function of D emerge:

$$L_{90\%} = 0.003D$$
$$L_{100\%} = 0.007D$$

Thus, for a viewing distance of 18 inches, the letter size specified by this formula would be 0.054 inches to be discernable by 90% of the population ($L_{90\%}$) and 0.126 inches to be discernable by 100% of the population ($L_{100\%}$). Type size is typically measured in points; there are approximately 72 points in an inch, making the appropriate type sizes four and nine points (i.e., 0.054 x 72 = 4, 0.126 x 72 = 9). In other words, 90% of the population should be able to discern four-point type at 18 inches and 100% of the population should be able to discern nine-point type at 18 inches.

Four-point type, however, is very small; this fact is an indication of the danger inherent in calculating type size without understanding type size conventions. These conventions were developed when type was cast in lead blocks and set in a printing press. A type font's specified size is the height of this block of lead. As shown in Figure 11.2, the font size will be greater than the height of an upper-case letter and much greater than the height of a lower-case letter. As a consequence, the results of the visual angle formula cannot be equated directly with a type's specified size.

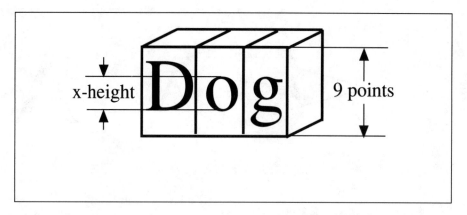

Figure 11.2. Type Size Versus Actual Letter Size. A type's size corresponds to the size of the block of lead in which the letters of that type would be cast. The height of a lower-case letter is thus substantially less than the specified size of the type. The x-height is the minimum height of a letter.

The height of the lower-case letter *x* (and *a*, *c*, *e*, and so on) is known as the x-height. If the visual angle formula is used, it is better to equate the results of that formula with the x-height of the letters in the font than with the font size itself. The visual angle specifies the minimum letter height that the human eye can discern; because the eye must discern these lower-case characters, they should not be smaller than the size specified by the visual angle. Poulton (1972) agrees that type size should be based on the x-height rather than the type size.

You should, however, remain wary of the visual angle formula even when it is applied to x-heights rather than point sizes. A variety of factors besides the x-height affect the apparent size of a typeface, including the width of the character strokes and the width of the letters themselves. Figure 11.3 shows how typefaces of an identical specified size appear to be different sizes. The issue is further complicated because the readability of type is also affected by the length of a line of type and the spacing between lines of type. All other things being equal, type will be more readable as spacing between lines is increased or as line length is reduced.

This is 12-point Times.

This is 12-point Helvetica.

This is 12-point Palatino.

This is 12-point New Century Schoolbook.

This is 12-point ITC Avant Garde Gothic Book.

Figure 11.3. Various Type Fonts of the Same Size. Even when various fonts are of the same specified size, there can be a difference in their apparent size.

The visual angle formula provides a useful starting point and can be very useful when type must be read from a greater-than-normal distance—for example, when determining the type size on a wall sign that is read at a distance of 10 feet. However, the formula ignores a number of relevant factors.

In fact, typesetters and writers seldom use a visual angle calculation when determining a type size. Instead, many prefer line lengths. Turnbull and Baird (1980) recommend that type size be based on a line length of one-and-a-half alphabets (i.e., a sequence of lower-case letters from *a* to *z* and then from *a* to *m* with no extra spaces), with two or three alphabets as a maximum line length and one alphabet as a minimum. A minimum line length is important because readability will suffer when lines become too short; the frequent transitions from the end of one line to the beginning of the next disrupt the reading process.

So, according to Turnbull and Baird, once the width of a procedure column is known, a type size should be chosen that allows one-and-a-half alphabets to fit on a line. However, this approach may present problems in multi-column procedures, where line length may be artificially shortened; in such a case, it would be a mistake to choose a type size so small that it would enable the procedure designer to squeeze one-and-a-half alphabets on a line in a single column.

The upshot of all of this is that determination of optimal type size, like so many other aspects of writing, is more of an art than a science (Hartley & Burnhill, 1977). As a general guideline, 12-point laser-printed text is a good, conservative starting point for text to be read from 18 inches. It is important to be conservative in the choice of type size because procedures may be read under inadequate lighting (e.g., a maintenance procedure performed locally). You should then be prepared to adjust your choice as necessary. If the line length is long, you should experiment by adding one or two points between lines, or by increasing type size. It is also important to address any comments that arise during validation and verification regarding type size and readability.

The final, and perhaps most useful, concern for determining type size is a subjective evaluation—can users read the procedure? If so, the type is fine. Be certain to have older users as well as younger users evaluate your choice of a type size because, in general, vision among older workers is poorer (Echeverria et al., in press). It is also important to evaluate type in the conditions under which it will be used, particularly if light levels are likely to be low. Finally, you should photocopy text in that type a few times (making copies of copies) to determine if legibility is maintained. For hand-held text, these subjective evaluations can be as useful, if not more useful, than the visual angle or line-length calculation.

Type Font

A type's appearance, or font, affects readability. As indicated in the preceding section, the appearance of different fonts varies greatly. And, also as stated in the previous section, the selection of a type font is more of an art than a science. Aesthetic criteria are typically sufficient to ensure that a type font is readable. Obviously, ornate or complex fonts should be avoided. Choose a font that is easy on the eye, and double-check your choice by consulting procedure users.

The biggest distinction in font appearance is between serif and sans serif fonts. Serif fonts include short lines at the ends of some of the lines that form the letter, as shown in Figure 11.4.

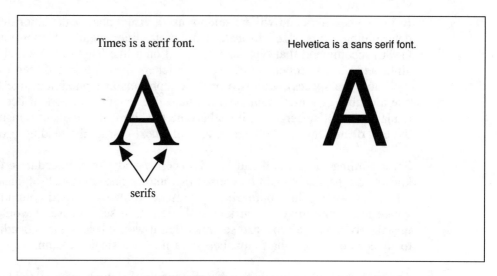

Figure 11.4. Serif and Sans Serif Fonts. Serifs are short lines at the end of the strokes in letters. *Sans* is French for *without*; hence, sans serif fonts are "without serifs."

Some authors (e.g., Mackh & Rew, 1991) consider serif typefaces to be easier to read, although, on the whole, the evidence is not conclusive (Barnes et al., 1989). Turnbull and Baird (1980, p. 86) describe the consensus in the field of typography:

> Typographers have long contended that legibility is maximized by the use of standard Roman [i.e., serif] faces. Tests to date have neither confirmed nor refuted this contention, although researchers have been inclined to conclude that it is valid. Typographers believe that familiarity and design factors render legibility to such faces. They point out that we learn to read from books printed in [serif type] and that the majority of what we read thereafter in books, magazines, and other literature is also printed in [serif type]. Further, the more irregular design features of [serif] faces help the reader grasp word forms more rapidly in the reading process than in [sans serif type]. Contrasting strokes give a rhythmic structure to words and serifs assist horizontal eye movement.

Often, however, the choice between a serif and a sans serif typeface is made aesthetically–sans serif typefaces often appear cleaner or more modern, while serif typefaces appear traditional (Benson, 1985).

In procedures, it may be best to stick with a serif typeface, such as the Times font used in the body of this document, because users are used to seeing serif type and may be less likely to object to it. An additional advantage of serif typefaces is that they are often easier to read on computer screens, thus reducing eye strain on procedure writers or word processing operators. However, sans serif typefaces can certainly be used in procedures, and should be used where a simpler typeface is desirable; for example, a sans serif typeface may be preferable in graphics, where the relatively simple type will not add to any clutter and distract the reader's attention from other elements of the graphic.

Type Case

Type case refers to whether the type is presented in all capitals, mixed case, or all lower case. For blocks of text, mixed case is easier to read than all capitals; thus, text in all capitals should be used sparingly in procedures (e.g., cautions should not be presented in all capitals). All capitals will not cause problems, however, for words appearing in isolation or in short phrases, such as emphasis of a single word.

A variety of studies have shown that blocks of text appearing in all capitals are difficult to read. Blocks of text written in mixed case are read approximately 12% faster than text written in all capitals (Tinker & Paterson, 1928; Tinker, 1955; Poulton & Brown, 1968; Hartley & Burnhill, 1977; Turnbull & Baird, 1980; Benson, 1985). According to Tinker (1955, p. 444), "The retarding effect of all-capital print is relatively large. In fact, few typographical variations in printing practice produce differences as large as this."

Figure 11.5 depicts the reason we have difficulty reading all capitals. When text is presented in mixed case, each word assumes a unique shape, which assists us in recognizing the word; when text is presented in all capitals, each word is a rectangle. Two other factors add to this effect: (1) all capitals occupy more space on the page, requiring our eye to physically cover more area and (2) we are accustomed to reading text in mixed case (Tinker & Paterson, 1928).

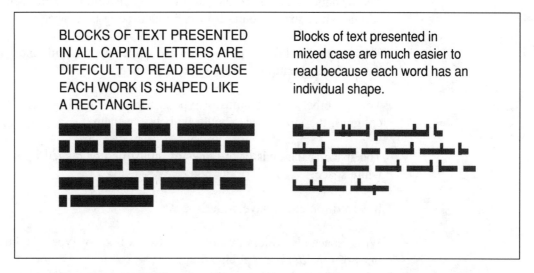

Figure 11.5. Blocks of Text Presented in Mixed Case Are Easier to Read. This figure shows two paragraphs, one in all capitals and the other in mixed case. The shaded areas beneath each paragraph depict the shapes of the words that comprise the paragraphs. In mixed case, words assume unique shapes, helping readers to recognize them. As a result, mixed case is easier to read than all capitals.

In some instances, however, it is beneficial to present text in all capital letters. Words in all capitals are larger than words in mixed case. This increased size allows readers to recognize *isolated* words in all capitals more quickly than in mixed case (Vartabedian, 1971). The key is that all capitals must be used sparingly (e.g., for conditional terms, cross-referencing terms, or equipment names) or else reading time will suffer, as discussed above.

11.2   Use white space according to the conventions of graphic design.

Summary

White space should be used to convey step structure, for emphasis (e.g., of step numbers or placekeeping aids), and for including meaningful line breaks (e.g., in conditional statements).

Discussion

White space is, as the name implies, the blank space on the page. It is one of the graphic designer's most powerful tools:

> White space frames content, separates ideas, defines sections, gives relief from print, and works with other visual markers to highlight information. It is simple to use and extremely effective. (Mackh & Rew, 1991, p. 210)

Parker (1988, p. 46) lists some of the many uses of white space:

- White space can open up the area surrounding a headline [or a heading]. The readability of a headline [or a heading] is often enhanced more by adding white space around it than by increasing type size.

- The margins of [a] . . . publication are white space. Wide margins push the reader's attention to the center of the page.

- The space between columns of type is white space. The wider the columns, the more space should be between them.

- The space at the ends of the lines of unjustified or ragged-right type is white space.

- Indented sentences have white space.

- White space also refers to the area between lines of type. Tightly packed lines of type *darken* a publication.

- White space can also be added between paragraphs to *open up* a publication.

White space is also one of the most misused tools of graphic design. One of the most common errors in page layout is to use inadequate white space. We have all seen documents that appear dense and cluttered; the problem often is that they lack adequate white space or have not used white space effectively.

The following sections discuss two forms of white space—line spacing and indentation.

Line Spacing

Line spacing in procedures results primarily when lines are skipped before and after steps or between items in lists. As shown in Figure 11.6, line spacing clearly differentiates steps and items in a list. (Lists will be discussed in Section 16.1).

[6]   Perform an autostart test of the emergency
         seal oil pump by performing the following:

     [6.1]   Depress pushbutton SON-P02 TEST
                HS-13B.   ___

     [6.2]   Observe that the red light goes on
                and the green light goes off.   ___

     [6.3]   Turn GEN SEAL OIL EMER PUMP P02,
                LON-HS-14 to STOP.   ___

     [6.4]   Observe that the red light goes off and
                the green light goes on.   ___

[7]   Turn on the turbine generator core monitor.   ___

[8]   Record the time that the core monitor was
         turned on in the control room log.   ___

Figure 11.6. Use of White Space. In this portion of a procedure, white space is used effectively by placing one blank line between each item in a list and two blank lines between each step. Indentation, another form of white space, is used to make step numbers and placekeeping aids stand out and to differentiate listed items from steps.

Line spacing can also be used to associate items. Note in Figure 11.6 how there is one blank line between items in a list and two blank lines between steps. This use of spacing associates the items in the list while differentiating steps (Hartley, 1985).

Indentation

Another way to use white space effectively is through indentation:

> One can consider the horizontal spacing of text [i.e., indentation] in much the same way as . . . [line] spacing. This is to say we can look to see how the [indentation] can be used to separate and group components of the text, and how one can vary the stopping point of . . . text in accord with its content rather than by using arbitrary rules about line lengths. (Hartley, 1985, p. 31)

In Figure 11.6, notice how the step numbers are separated from the text of the step so that subsequent lines of text align with the beginning of the first line of the step or the listed item. This use of indentation gives the step a particular shape that can help users quickly locate the step and identify it by number. Additional indentation is used to indicate that listed items are subordinate to the steps that contain them. Computer programmers frequently use indentation in this manner to simplify the structure of the code they write (Green, 1977). Finally, indentation is used to make the placekeeping aid stand out on the right margin. Compare Figure 11.6 with Figure 11.7, which fails to use indentation.

Indentation can also be controlled by establishing rules for ending lines of type (Hartley, 1985). For example, line breaks in conditional statements can be positioned so that a line break occurs after each clause, as shown in Figure 11.8. There are advantages to this approach that may make the step easier to comprehend (Hartley, 1982). One is that the conditional terms are emphasized by consistently being at the start of a line, as well as by full capitalization and underlining. Another advantage is that the two conditions are clearly differentiated from each other, and from the action, by the line breaks.

[6]   Perform an autostart test of the emergency seal
        oil pump by performing the following:

[6.1]   Depress pushbutton SON-P02 TEST
        HS-13B.   ___

[6.2]   Observe that the red light goes on and the
        green light goes off.   ___

[6.3]   Turn GEN SEAL OIL EMER PUMP P02,
        LON-HS-14 to STOP.   ___

[6.4]   Observe that the red light goes off and green
        light goes on.   ___

[7]   Turn on the turbine generator core monitor.   ___

[8]   Record the time that the core monitor was turned
        on in the control room log.   ___

Figure 11.7. Ineffective Use of Horizontal White Space. Here, horizontal white space is not used effectively. As a result, placekeeping aids and step numbers do not stand out readily and it is difficult to match listed items to steps.

[5]   <u>WHEN</u> the main turbine is at rated speed
        <u>AND</u> turbine oil temperature has been stable
        for 20 minutes,
        <u>THEN</u> return temperature control to automatic.

Figure 11.8. Line Breaks in a Logic Statement. Here, line breaks are inserted after each clause in a conditional statement. These line breaks can make the step easier to understand.

11.3   Use ragged-right margins.

Summary

Right-justified text is more difficult to read than ragged-right text because of the variation among the spaces between words necessary to justify the right margin. For this reason, ragged-right margins should be used in procedures.

Discussion

Practically all text is left-justified, meaning that all lines begin the same distance from the left margin. The right margin is a different matter. If text is right-justified, all lines end the same distance from the right margin. The spaces between the words (and sometimes between letters) in a line are varied to adjust the length of that line. If text is ragged right, lines are of unequal length; no attempt is made to adjust line length. The text you are reading now is ragged right. Figure 11.9 shows the different forms of justification.

This text is left-justified and ragged right, which is the alignment preferred in procedures. This text is left-justified and ragged right, which is the alignment preferred in procedures.	This text is right-justified and left-justified. This text is right-justified and left-justified. This text is right-justified and left-justified.
This text is right-justified and ragged left. Avoid this uncommon combination. This text is right-justified and ragged left. Avoid this uncommon combination.	This text is centered (i.e., ragged right and ragged left). This text is centered (i.e., ragged right and ragged left). This text is centered (i.e., ragged right and ragged left).

Figure 11.9. Justification. There are four ways that type can be justified.

Right-justified text can be more difficult to read because the varying spaces between words can be distracting. Hyphenation is often used to break words between lines, thus allowing more control over the spaces between words; but hyphenated words can also be more difficult to read, so the net effect is not likely to be an improvement. Trollip and Sales (1986) found that, although there were no differences in comprehension between right-justified and ragged-right text, the right-justified text was read more slowly. Other researchers also recommend ragged-right margins (Benson, 1985; Hartley & Burnhill, 1977; Turnbull & Baird, 1980).

Yet, right-justified text is quite common in books and newspapers. Why is right justification successful to these situations, yet problematic in others? The answer is that the capabilities of the device used to print a document and the length of a line can reduce the variation in space between words, making sentences easier to read.

Expensive typesetting machines are capable of varying the space between letters as well as the space between words. Differences in letter spacing, which are too small to be noticed themselves, can smooth out the distracting, noticeable variations among word spaces. Books and newspaper publishers use these typesetting machines, and can thus produce right-justified text that is readable. Other output devices, such as most daisy-wheel printers, dot-matrix printers, and laser printers, cannot vary letter spacing as effectively, so procedure writers do not have these techniques at their disposal.

Line length also affects the readability of right-justified text. In a longer line, the space that must be added can be divided among more spaces; in shorter lines, there are fewer word spaces to which this extra space can be added; hence, the spaces become proportionally larger.

Short line lengths are especially likely to be problematic in multi-column procedures. Even with longer line lengths, there are no benefits to right justification that outweigh the potential loss in readability. Consequently, right justification should not be used in procedures.

Ragged-left text, incidentally, should be avoided in all procedures. When we read, it is easier if our eyes return to a common anchor point as we reach the end of a line of text. In left-justified text, this anchor point is always in the same place—a given distance from the left margin. If the text is ragged left, we must hunt for the beginning of a line, as its location will vary. Reading is impeded. The same problem occurs with centered text, although it is permissible to center one- or two-line figure captions.

Chapter 12

Placekeeping

This chapter discusses placekeeping aids, which are boxes or blanks that users check as they perform a step. Placekeeping aids can also be referred to as check-offs. It presents one principle.

12.1 Provide placekeeping aids to help users track their progress through the procedure.

Summary

Provide usable placekeeping aids for all actions in procedures. It may also be useful to provide placekeeping aids for conditions in conditional statements.

Discussion

Placekeeping aids are blank lines or boxes that appear with each step or each action in a step. Users check the placekeeping aid as they perform the step or the action, tracking their progress through the procedure. Placekeeping aids prevent duplication or omission of actions and help users find their place if execution of the procedure is interrupted. Placekeeping aids are important in all types of procedures, and become critical when procedures include cross-references (see Chapter 19), as users are likely to lose their place as they move from one procedure to another. Users can also use tables of contents, tabs, and ribbon markers to help trace their progress through the procedure.

In some procedures, placekeeping aids also serve an administrative function, by providing a record of the procedure's execution. These procedures are archived and may be checked at a later date. For example, maintainers may be required to initial a step instructing them to torque a bolt to specifications. An initial signifies that the bolt was torqued correctly, and may be checked at a later date if a question arises. Critical activities may require independent verification by a second person and a second set of initials.

Some steps contain more than one action. In these instances, it is a sound practice to provide a placekeeping aid for each action, as shown in Figure 12.1. Depending on facility administrative practices and user expectations, it may or may not be appropriate to include a placekeeping aid for the step as a whole. Figure 12.1 does not include a placekeeping aid for the introductory conditional statement, on the logic that such a placekeeping aid is redundant; once the three placekeeping aids for the actions are checked, the step has been performed. In some cases, however, users prefer to see a placekeeping aid for the entire step; in others, facility administrative requirements may specify that such a placekeeping aid be used.

---

[19] IF no RCPs are running,
THEN check that the following criteria are met:

    [19.1] RCS ΔT is less than 10°F.   —

    [19.2] RCS T_c is between 552 and 568°F.   —

    [19.3] RCS is at least 28°F subcooled based
           on T_h RTD.   —

Figure 12.1. Placekeeping Aids for Multiple Actions. The placekeeping aids are the lines along the right margin. This example includes a placekeeping aid for each action, rather than a placekeeping aid for the step as a whole, allowing users to verify the performance of each action.

Placekeeping aids may also be useful for conditions in conditional statements, as shown in Figure 12.2.

---

[1] IF all of the following conditions exist:

  • Pressure in at least 1 steam
    generator is decreasing   —

  • RCS pressure is decreasing   —

  • Containment radiation is stable —

THEN use this procedure.   —

Figure 12.2. Use of Placekeeping Aids for Conditions in a Conditional Statement. Users may mark placekeeping aids if the conditions are met, reducing demands on short-term memory.

Placekeeping aids should be located so that they are surrounded by white space and so that they are easily associated with the items to which they correspond. The best locations are either along the left margin, beside the step number, or the right margin.

Chapter 13

Emphasis Techniques

Emphasis techniques are typographical, graphical, spatial, and verbal cues that visually distinguish information within a body of text. Typographical emphasis techniques include:

- **bolding**

- *italicizing*

- <u>underlining</u>

- ALL CAPITALS

- [brackets]

- "quotation marks"

Figure 13.1 demonstrates the use of typographic emphasis, specifically all capitals and bolding.

---

[55]   Ensure:

- PRIMARY CIRCUIT BREAKER - Switch **on**

- POWER ON 480 VAC - Green light **on**

- RIGHT DOOR CLOSED - Amber light and switch **on**

- HOIST UP MAXIMUM - Green light **on**

Figure 13.1. Emphasis Techniques. Here, the emphasis techniques of capitalization, bolding, and indentation are used effectively.

Graphical emphasis techniques include framing, shading, or coloring. Cautions, for example, can be framed.

Spatial emphasis techniques refer to the use of white space to surround the item that is emphasized. Emphasis occurs because the item contrasts with the blank space surrounding it. Section 11.2 discusses the use of white space. Consistent placement of something on the page is also a spatial emphasis technique; for example, the procedure name could appear at the top of each page.

Verbal emphasis techniques include the use of identifying terms, such as *Important*, *NOTE*, or *Caution!*.

This chapter presents one principle.

13.1   Consistently use emphasis techniques to code and highlight information.

Summary

Emphasis techniques should be used consistently throughout a text to code and highlight specific types of information. Avoid overemphasis.

Discussion

Emphasis techniques, such as bolding or the use of white space, are frequently misused in procedures. This section discusses the use of emphasis techniques. It begins by distinguishing between true emphasis and coding, and explains how emphasis techniques should be minimized and used consistently.

Emphasis Versus Coding

Emphasis techniques, when implemented correctly, actually perform two functions:

- They let the reader know that something is important. This is known as *true emphasis*.

- They let the reader know what something is (e.g., if something is in a box, then it is a caution). This is known as *coding*.

These two functions differ and, often, the coding function is more important than the true emphasis function.

True emphasis techniques make something appear important because of the visual difference between the emphasized item and its surroundings. The reader's eye is drawn to the word or section that stands out from its surroundings.

True emphasis techniques make things stand out on the procedure page. Something should stand out for one of two reasons: so readers will see it when scanning the page or so readers will realize that it is important. Headings, for example, should stand out so a reader scanning the procedure can quickly locate a particular section. It may also be useful for control panel markings or equipment labels to stand out when quoted in the procedure, so the user can quickly locate the label when looking back at the procedure to verify that the label corresponds to the label cited in the procedure. True emphasis can also be used to indicate importance, but this should be done with care because, in a terse procedure, every word is important. When emphasis is used to indicate importance, overemphasis, as discussed in the next section, can be a danger, because almost every word in a procedure can be considered important for one reason or another.

But emphasis techniques do more than highlight important information. Emphasis techniques also code, or identify, information. For example, if all warnings are printed in red ink, the reader can identify a warning at the first notice of red printing.

Coding is important. The emphasis of conditional terms, for example, serves as more of a coding function than a true emphasis function. Consider the following conditional statement:

> <u>IF</u> you have less than 50 ml of the sample
> <u>OR</u> you have less than 1 hour to complete the test,
> <u>THEN</u> GO TO Attachment 2, Measuring SR-89 and SR-90 in Air Samples.

The conditional terms <u>IF</u>, <u>OR</u>, and <u>THEN</u> are capitalized and underlined not simply because they are important to understanding the step. Granted, the step would be difficult to understand if any of these words were missing, but it would also be difficult to understand if almost any other word were missing. The primary reason that these words are emphasized uniquely is to mark (or code) the parts of the conditional statement. When the user sees <u>IF</u>, he knows the condition of a conditional statement follows; when he sees <u>OR</u>, he knows that another condition follows and that either one or both of the conditions must be true; when he sees <u>THEN</u>, he knows that the action that is contingent on the preceding conditions will follow. The conditional terms function as labels for the various parts of the conditional statement.

Use of Emphasis Techniques

Whether used for true emphasis or coding, emphasis techniques should be minimized and used consistently. Users should know what the various emphasis techniques mean.

Emphasis is relative; true emphasis techniques work because they contrast with their surroundings. If emphasis techniques are overused, then the "emphasized" information has no subdued surroundings to contrast against. The result is that nothing is emphasized, as illustrated in Figure 13.2.

★★★★★★★★★★★★★★NOTE★★★★★★★★★★★★★★★

☞ [Eight hours operating fuel *required* **by the NFPA.**]
<u>Fuel consumption</u> for this engine per the
Manufacturer's Specifications is
14 gal/h under NORMAL LOAD CONDITIONS, or 112 gal/8h.
•**Minimum** *allowable fuel level* is <u>120 gal</u>.

★★★★★★★★★★★★★★★★★★★★★★★★★★★★★★

Figure 13.2. Overuse of Emphasis. When everything is emphasized, nothing is emphasized. This (admittedly exaggerated) example demonstrates how overemphasized text can be distracting and unprofessional, if not downright confusing.

Overuse will also detract from emphasis techniques that are used to code information. For effective coding, the user should be able to distinguish the different techniques used. If too many techniques are used, the user will not be able to keep track of them all. Once this happens, the coding techniques contribute little more than clutter and confusion.

It is also necessary to use emphasis techniques consistently in order to transfer this qualitative information to the reader. If, for example, equipment names are italicized in the first section of a procedure but not throughout the remainder of the procedure, the reader's speed and understanding may decrease as he or she scans unsuccessfully for a component name in italic print. Important information might be overlooked with this type of inconsistency. Inconsistent coding will lead to confusion, decrease reading speed, and increase the potential for misinterpretations.

Users should be trained to understand the ways in which emphasis techniques are used. Research suggests that typographical emphasis is most effective when the reader knows in advance what the various cues mean (Hartley & Burnhill, 1977; Glynn, Britton, & Tillman, 1985). This information can be provided during organized training for the procedure or within the procedure text. Within the text, for example, an introductory section can be provided that states which emphasis techniques are used and what each one represents, such as, *In this procedure, action verbs are printed in bold lettering, warnings are printed in red, and equipment names are italicized.* A better approach, however, might be to ensure that users are trained on this critical information.

Graphical and Verbal Emphasis Techniques

A complete discussion of graphical emphasis techniques is beyond the scope of this book. A few general caveats are presented here. Background shading should be avoided because it reduces contrast between the type and the background, making the type more difficult to read, particularly if the procedure has been photocopied. Color can be highly effective for emphasis, but it is difficult to produce colored documents. Color can easily be misused; we have probably all seen color computer screens that are distracting and even ugly. Icons or symbols can also be used effectively as emphasis techniques; for example, a radiation symbol could be used to mark steps where users are working with radioactive material. Such icons will be most effective if users understand their meaning.

Verbal emphasis techniques in procedures are generally restricted to headings on cautions and notes. As with other emphasis techniques, verbal emphasis techniques are most useful when their use is minimized; if every step is marked *Danger!*, users will quickly come to ignore the warning.

Coding Revisions to Procedures: An Example

Many procedures are living documents, meaning that they are updated as the need arises. It is important to draw users' attention to any changes in the procedure so they will be aware of changes and will not perform the procedure the old way out of habit. This subsection discusses the criteria that affect the choice of a coding technique for alerting users to revised information and provides an example of the types of factors that a procedure writer should consider when deciding whether a coding or emphasis technique is appropriate and, if so, which technique should be used.

The technique used to identify revised information should not be intrusive, or it may conflict with other emphasis and coding techniques. Bold type, for example, would be a poor choice for this purpose, as a substantially revised procedure would have page after page of bold type, which would not only be difficult to read, but would overwhelm any other emphasis and coding techniques that were used. In fact, most forms of typographical coding would probably be unacceptable, given the rather extensive use of typographical techniques for other purposes. Similarly, spatial emphasis techniques are also likely to be of little use, as spatial coding (i.e., white space) is used rather extensively for other purposes. Verbal techniques are also likely to be intrusive, as the use of words to identify new information would grow tiresome to the reader, particularly if they were incorporated in the step (e.g., *Revised step: Trip the 4.2 kv breakers*).

Graphic emphasis techniques, however, are better suited for identifying revisions. One graphic technique is, in fact, widely used to indicate revised portions of procedures—the change bar. A change bar is a vertical bar that appears near the right or left margin and is aligned with text that has been revised. Being off to the side, the change bar is not intrusive, even if it runs down the entire page, indicating that the entire page has been revised. Yet, it still effectively alerts users to revisions. Figure 13.3 shows a change bar.

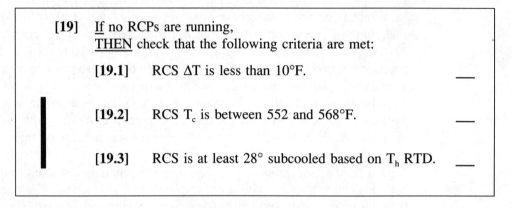

Figure 13.3. Change Bar. The horizontal bar in the left margin indicates that items **[19.2]** and **[19.3]** have been changed since the last version of the procedure.

Chapter 14

Procedure Organization

This chapter presents four principles regarding procedure organization:

- Organize procedures in a hierarchical, logical, consistent manner and reveal that organization to users through the use of headings.

- Use step numbering and structure that provides useful information to users and is not overly complex.

- Use appendices and attachments to present information that would otherwise be difficult to integrate into the procedure.

- Include adequate identification information in procedures.

14.1 Organize procedures in a hierarchical, logical, consistent manner and reveal that organization to users through the use of headings.

Summary

Procedures should be organized hierarchically; that is, related steps should be grouped into sections. These sections should be given names that reflect their content. Headings should be emphasized in a manner that makes them stand out and that provides progressively less emphasis to lower-level headings. Tables of contents should be included in procedures that are more than a few pages long.

Discussion

Many researchers emphasize the importance of organization. Jonassen (1982, p. 10) says, "The stronger the organization of the text, the more likely it will be assimilated by the reader. . . . *The importance of organization to text cannot be denied*" [author's italics]. Meyer (1985, p. 70) makes a similar point: "Research shows that a communication is vastly more efficient (it saves effort) and effective (it gets results) if it follows a plan rather than being a miscellaneous sequence of sentences or paragraphs." Although procedures are not presented in paragraphs, Meyer's point certainly remains applicable—the procedure should not be a miscellaneous collection of steps.

In all procedures, the overall organizational scheme will be dictated by the order in which steps are performed. Clearly, the steps that must be performed first should appear first in the procedure. Prerequisites, such as a list of tools that will be needed or a set of conditions that must be met before the procedure is executed, should appear before steps. However, organization is more than the sequence of the steps; it also applies to how steps are grouped into sections. Through the effective use of sections and the effective identification of those sections by headings, much information can be imparted to the procedure user.

The importance of a hierarchical structure

Many researchers believe that a hierarchical structure is best for presenting procedures (Bovair & Kieras, 1989; Fuchs, Engelschall, & Imlay, 1981, Huckin; 1983). Hierarchical procedures are easier to comprehend (Dixon, 1987) and to learn and remember (Holland, Charrow, & Wright, 1988, p. 35): "If procedures are to be learned and remembered, then hierarchical structure appears to be essential."

According to *The Random House Dictionary of the English Language* (1967, p. 669), a hierarchy is "any system of persons or things ranked one above another." Hierarchical structures are very common. Businesses, for example, are often organized hierarchically, with a president at the top of the hierarchy, the vice presidents beneath him or her, middle managers beneath the vice presidents, and so on. Figure 14.1 shows how procedures can also be organized hierarchically.

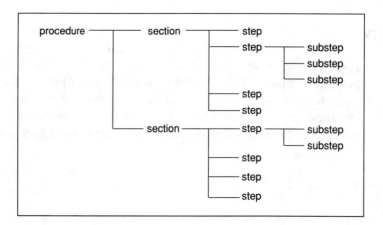

Figure 14.1. Procedure Hierarchy. In a hierarchical procedure, procedures consist of sections, which consist of steps, some of which include substeps.

In procedures, the opposite of a clearly revealed hierarchy is an unstructured list of steps. Figure 14.2 depicts an unstructured list.

---

[1]   Depress EMER BEARING OIL PUMP TEST SWITCH A,
LON HS-52A.   ___

[2]   Observe that the red light goes on and the green light
goes off.   ___

[3]   Take EMER BEARING OIL PUMP P05, LON-HS-8,
to STOP.   ___

[4]   Observe that the red light goes off and the green light
goes on.   ___

[5]   Ensure that the emergency seal oil pump is in standby.   ___

[6]   Depress pushbutton SON-P02 TEST HS-13B.   ___

[7]   Observe that the red light goes on and the green light
goes off.   ___

[8]   Take GEN SEAL OIL EMER PUMP P02,
LON-HS-14 to stop.   ___

[9]   Observe that the red light goes off and the green light
goes on.   ___

Figure 14.2. An Unstructured List of Procedure Steps. No attempt is made to group these steps. Compare with Figure 14.3.

Figure 14.3 revises Figure 14.2 by grouping many of these actions as listed items beneath a descriptive higher-level step.

[1]   Perform an autostart test of the emergency bearing oil
             pump by completing the following:

    [1.1]   Depress EMER BEARING OIL PUMP TEST
                         SWITCH A, LON HS-52A.   —

    [1.2]   Observe that the red light goes on and the
                         green light goes off.   —

    [1.3]   Take EMER BEARING OIL PUMP P05,
                         LON-HS-8, to STOP.   —

    [1.4]   Observe that the red light goes off and the
                         green light goes on.   —

[2]   Ensure that the emergency seal oil pump is in standby.   —

[3]   Perform an autostart test of the emergency seal oil
             pump by performing the following:

    [3.1]   Depress pushbutton SON-P02 TEST HS-13B.   —

    [3.2]   Observe that the red light goes on and the
                         green light goes off.   —

    [3.3]   Take GEN SEAL OIL EMER PUMP P02,
                         LON-HS-14 to stop.   —

    [3.4]   Observe that the red light goes off and the
                         green light goes on.   —

Figure 14.3. Grouping Used to Show the Hierarchy of Actions. This figure revises
Figure 14.2 to group steps beneath upper-level steps that summarize the actions that follow
(e.g., *Perform an autostart test of the emergency seal oil pump by performing the
following:*).[1]

Although Figure 14.3 depicts a portion of the hierarchy at the step level, the same
principles of organization apply when combining steps into sections—namely,
related steps should be grouped into sections and the name of these sections should
reflect the common theme in the steps.

---

[1]Figures 14.2 and 14.3 deal with steps rather than sections for the simple reason that steps
are more concise; it would have required too much space to show an example of a series
of steps that were grouped into sections. But the same principle applies.

Headings

Headings present the names of sections. As discussed in the following sections, headings help readers comprehend and access text:

- Headings help readers comprehend a procedure by providing information that they can link to information they already know. For instance, the heading *Main Turbine Start-Up* tells the reader that the steps in that section deal with start-up of the main turbine (Hartley & Jonassen, 1985).

- Headings serve as access aids by helping readers locate information in a procedure. If the procedure user is looking for the steps that will start the main turbine, the heading *Main Turbine Start-Up* indicates where those steps begin in the procedure. Access aids are especially important in cross-referencing. Note that, for headings to effectively aid in access, it is important that they be emphasized so that they stand out on the page (Hartley & Jonassen, 1985).

In a hierarchical document, headings can be referred to by their levels. A first-level heading is at the highest position in the hierarchy. In this book, first-level headings identify Parts One, Two, Three, and so on. Second-level headings are lower in the hierarchy; in this document, second-level headings identify chapters. This pattern continues through the lowest level of the hierarchy.

Headings should provide specific, useful information to readers (Hartley & Jonassen, 1985). For this reason, vague headings like *Action Steps* should be avoided. Instead, headings should describe the content of the section; for example, a series of headings such as *Turning Gear Operation*, *Turbine Warming Operations*, and *Turbine Start-Up* provides more information than the single heading *Action Steps*.

Headings Facilitate Comprehension

Headings help readers comprehend information by providing a context for that information. Consider the following passage, which is presented without a heading (Anderson et al., 1977, p. 373):

> Rocky slowly got up from the mat, planning his escape. He hesitated a moment and thought. Things were not going well. What bothered him most was being held, especially since the charge against him had been weak. He considered his present situation. The lock that held him was strong but he thought he could break it. He knew, however, that his timing would have to be perfect. Rocky was aware that it was because of much of his earlier roughness that he was being penalized so severely—much too severely from his point of view. The situation was becoming frustrating; the pressure had been grinding on him for too long. He was being ridden unmercifully. Rocky was getting angry now. He felt

he was ready to make his move. He knew that his success or failure
would depend on what he did in the next few seconds.

What is this passage about? Suppose that it had been preceded by the title, *The
Wrestling Match*. Read it again with that title in mind. Now suppose that it was
preceded by a different title—*Escape from Alcatraz*. Read the passage again. This
example demonstrates the power of headings in shaping the way that readers will
perceive writing.

However, it could be argued that this passage is not a realistic example. Anderson
et al.'s (1977) research on headings, from which this passage is drawn, does set up
a straw man, in the form of a deliberately ambiguous passage. Hartley and
Jonassen (1985, pp. 240-241) discuss one of Anderson's earlier experiments in this
regard:

> The effectiveness of headings needs to be affirmed with natural, less
> ambiguous prose . . . . Few studies have examined this question posed in
> this particular form.

Thus, this example should not be considered strong evidence on the ability of
headings to facilitate comprehension. However, other evidence suggests that
headings do help readers understand what they read. Huckin (1983, p. 97) is
convinced of the support in the research for the notion that headings aid in
comprehension, stating that "many psychological studies have demonstrated the
powerful effect of headings and subheadings on comprehension." Spyridakis and
Standal (1987) found that headings did aid in comprehension, producing the
greatest effects when a passage was neither too easy nor too difficult for its
readers. Further, the notion that headings aid comprehension is somewhat
buttressed by studies that have found that headings that have no relation to or are
contrary to the text adversely affect comprehension (Hartley & Jonassen, 1985).
On the other hand, Spyridakis (1989b) found that headings had no effect on
immediate recall. She expected this, "based on much of the literature that has
failed to find immediate effects for headings" (p. 410).

Obviously, the research does not clearly point in one direction, and perhaps never
will. However, these results should by no means discourage writers from using
headings. Spyridakis and Standal (1987, p. 294) sum up the issue nicely:
"Because there is ample reason to believe that signals [i.e., headings] help and no
reason to believe that they hinder, it seems reasonable to suggest that a reader may
be best served through the inclusion of [headings]."

Headings Facilitate Access

There is little question that headings help readers locate parts of a document. Mackh and Rew (1991, p. 211) explain how headings facilitate access: "Headings flag information for readers, helping them to scan and locate sections quickly. They act as mini-overviews, indicating what information is contained within document sections and subsections."

A consistent organizational scheme will also facilitate access. If the first few sections of every procedure are (for instance) *Introduction*, *Precautions and Limitations*, and *Prerequisite Instructions*, users will be able to locate these sections more easily. The writers' guide should specify these generic procedure sections or should provide criteria that procedure writers can use when dividing a procedure into sections.

Headings can also facilitate access during cross-referencing. It is often best to refer users to an entire section rather than a series of steps, because a section is a logical unit of information. Most cross-references should be to complete sections.

Format for Headings

Brusaw, Alred, and Oliu (1987, p. 293) say that "there is no correct format" for headings. Experimental findings bear this out. Hartley (1985) found that position and form of headings made no significant difference in the headings' effectiveness. Hartley and Trueman (1983) found that position of headings made no difference. Thus, much is left to the writers' discretion regarding the format and position of headings. What is important is that (1) headings are emphasized so that they stand out and (2) upper-level headings are emphasized more heavily than lower-level headings.

A variety of techniques emphasize headings. Headings may be surrounded by white space, bolded, italicized, underlined, fully capitalized, initially capitalized, or set in a larger font. Generally, no one of these techniques is any better or any worse than any other. However, these emphasis techniques should be used in combinations that convey the hierarchy of the headings; in other words, in a document with four levels of headings, first-level headings should have the most emphasis, second-level headings should have less emphasis, third-level headings even less, and fourth-level headings should have the least emphasis. Figure 14.4 shows one way of placing progressively less emphasis on each level of heading.

Level	Centered	All Capitals	Bold	Blank Line Before and After
First	X	X	X	X
Second		X	X	X
Third			X	X
Fourth				X

Figure 14.4. Hierarchical Emphasis of Headings. The combination of emphasis techniques shown provides progressively less emphasis to each level of heading.

It is often tempting to include more levels of headings than will be useful to readers; writers often feel the need to include fifth- or even sixth-level headings in documents. Many researchers warn against this. Brusaw, Alred, and Oliu (1987, p. 289) write, "In extremely technical material as many as five levels of [headings] may be appropriate, but as a general rule it is rarely necessary (and usually confusing) to use more than three." The problem is that readers cannot keep track of a detailed hierarchy of headings, so the headings wind up conveying some global, complex scheme that is evident only to the writer.

Tables of Contents

Headings are typically listed in a table of contents. While it is a good idea to include a table of contents in any procedure that is more than a few pages long, writers should be aware that users refer to tables of contents and indexes only 25 percent of the time (Sticht, 1985), so it is not a good idea to rely on them. Procedures should include other means of helping readers locate information; these include properly emphasized headings, which will stand out as readers scan the pages of the procedure, and tabs to indicate section breaks for long procedures.

Several concerns govern the design of a table of contents (Wright, 1985). Readers should be able to easily link the table of contents' entries with corresponding page numbers. A horizontal line of periods is often used between the entry and the page number for this reason. A table of contents should reflect the hierarchical organization of a document; in other words, first-level headings in the table of contents should be emphasized more heavily than lower-level headings.

14.2   Use step numbering and structure that provides useful information to users and is not overly complex.

Summary

Step numbers should be formatted so that they indicate that a step is to follow, they should uniquely identify steps, and they should provide information regarding the location of the step in the hierarchy of the procedure, unless this information is provided in another manner. Hierarchical step numbering should not be overused.

Discussion

Steps are numbered for three reasons: (1) a step number indicates an item in a procedure is a step; (2) step numbers identify individual steps, which facilitates cross-referencing; and (3) step numbers can indicate how sections, steps, and substeps are related. When numbering steps, or other information in procedures, it is important to keep these purposes in mind so that the step numbering scheme is useful and is not too complex for the procedure. Figure 14.5 depicts effective step numbering.

[6]	Perform an autostart test of the emergency seal oil pump by performing the following:
[6.1]	Depress pushbutton SON-P02 TEST HS-13B.
[6.2]	Observe that the red light goes on and the green light goes off.
[6.3]	Turn GEN SEAL OIL EMER PUMP P02, LON-HS-14 to STOP.
[6.4]	Observe that the red light goes off and green light goes on.
[7]	Turn on the turbine generator core monitor.
[8]	Record the time that the core monitor was turned on in the control room log.

Figure 14.5. Effective Step Numbering. This figure demonstrates one method of effectively numbering steps. Note that step numbers are surrounded by brackets and bolded to differentiate them from other items that may be numbered, such as headings.

Procedure users should readily recognize the steps in a procedure as steps. A step number is one cue that a step, and thus an action, is to follow. Unique identification of steps allows users to differentiate the essential directions from supporting information. Other information in the procedure, such as background information, should not be numbered in the same manner as a step, or the information may be confused with a step. If these items are numbered, step numbers could be surrounded by square brackets, for example, to differentiate them from other numbered items.

Step numbers also help users find specific steps. Identification of specific steps is particularly important in cross-referencing. Users must be told in an unambiguous manner which step they are going to. One means of accomplishing this is to use a hierarchial step numbering scheme. In such a scheme, the third step in Section 5 is Step 5.3, the first step in Section 12 is Step 12.1, and so on. Under this scheme, each step in the procedure will have a unique number, so a cross-reference to, say, Step 17.1 will unambiguously denote a specific location in the procedure.

Hierarchical step numbering also provides useful information to users regarding the relationship of the step to the overall procedure; when a user sees Step 4.3, he knows that it is in Section 4. This knowledge can provide information on the context under which the step is being executed. Research indicates that hierarchical step numbering can provide useful information to procedure users (Benson, 1985). The NRC (1982) recommends that step numbers be used hierarchically.

Hierarchial step numbering is not the only means of providing this information; for example, a section title repeated at the top of the page will also provide this information, perhaps more clearly than a step number, because users do not have to associate the first part of the hierarchical number with a section title. In other words, it is easier to attach a useful meaning to *1.0 Immediate Operator Actions (continued)* at the top of the page than to remember that the *1* in Step 1.23 corresponds to the immediate operator actions section.

It is quite possible to carry the notion of hierarchical step numbering too far. Figure 14.6 shows an excerpt from a computer procedure where hierarchical step numbering has been overused. Consider Items 5.1.1.2.1 and 5.1.1.2.2 in Figure 14.6. What purpose is accomplished in numbering them? The number is not an indication that actions follow, because headings, steps, and listed items are numbered according to an identical format. The numbers would not be an aid to cross-referencing, as there would be no justifiable reason to cross-reference to so brief and fragmentary a piece of information as *a delay in delivery to data entry*. Finally, the numbers do not convey any useful hierarchical information, as it is obvious from indentation and context that Items 5.1.1.2.1 and 5.1.1.2.2 are subsumed under Item 5.1.1.2. Further, the hierarchical information presented is not useful to the user, who should not be expected to remember that items 5.1.1.2.1 and 5.1.1.2.2 are subsumed under item 5.1.1.2, which is in turn subsumed under *Discrepancies in Turnaround Time*, which is subsumed under *Run Date and*

Date Keyed, which is subsumed under *Interpreting Discrepancies*. The hierarchy is too complex; it goes five levels deep in half a page.

5.0   Interpreting Discrepancies

    5.1   Run Date and Date Keyed

        5.1.1   Discrepancies in Turnaround Time

            5.1.1.1 If the run date is equal to or just slightly greater than the date the client information sheet went to data entry, then the system is functioning properly.

            5.1.1.2 If the run date is several days greater than the date the client information sheet went to data entry, at least one of the following conditions exists:

                5.1.1.2.1   a delay in delivery to data entry

                5.1.1.2.2   a problem at the data entry level

---

Figure 14.6. Overuse of the Hierarchical Numbering Scheme. The hierarchical numbering scheme as used here serves no useful purpose at the lower levels of the hierarchy. No benefit is realized by numbering Items 5.1.1.2.1 and 5.1.1.2.2 (adapted from Horn & Kelly, 1981, p. 18).

When overused, a hierarchical numbering scheme makes the procedure seem more complex and cluttered. A hierarchial numbering scheme can also waste space due to the excessive indentation required. Procedure writers should consider using bullets, placekeeping aids, or a simpler identification scheme (e.g., a, b, c) if a hierarchical numbering scheme is not serving a useful function.

As an aside, there are superior formats for presenting the type of information in Figure 14.6. A flowchart or decision table would be superior for presenting this type of diagnostic criteria. Section 20.4 discusses the advantages of flowcharts.

14.3   Use appendices and attachments to present information that would otherwise be difficult to integrate into the procedure.

Summary

Appendices and attachments can be used to present information that cannot be easily incorporated in the procedure, such as contingency actions, actions performed by someone other than the procedure reader, and periodic steps. Because transitions to appendices and attachments are disruptive to readers, the use of appendices and attachments should be minimized.

Discussion

There is no universal distinction between the terms *attachment* and *appendix*, although some facilities do distinguish between them. Because this distinction can be confusing, it is not recommended that you distinguish between appendices and attachments unless necessary. In the remainder of this section, we will use only the term *appendix*.

The following types of information may be included in an appendix:

- Appendices can include lengthy sequences of contingency actions that are not normally performed when the procedure is executed. In an appendix, these actions are out of the way but available should they be needed. They would be accessed via a conditional cross-reference (see Chapter 19). Frequently performed actions should not be included in appendices, however, unless they meet other criteria expressed in this section.

- Appendices can include actions that are performed by someone other than the person who is using the procedure, allowing the person who will be using the appendix to remove it from the procedure.

- Appendices can include steps that are performed repeatedly, allowing the user to refer to the appendix periodically.

- Appendices can include data sheets and other lengthy forms that would be difficult to incorporate in the procedure.

- Appendices can present supplementary and background information that may be useful to procedure users.

- Figures can be included in appendices; however, figures should be placed in appendices with care, as users are much more likely to refer to graphics that are on the same page as the portion of the procedure that refers to them (or on the facing page).

These are all useful functions for appendices; however, the danger in using appendices is that it is often easier to shove something into an appendix than to figure out where it really belongs within the organization of the procedure. Figures, for example, are commonly included in appendices because they are difficult to incorporate into the procedure at the appropriate point. Similarly, it is often easier to include a series of steps in an appendix than it is to revise a procedure to include those steps where they really belong. These are practices that benefit the procedure writer and hurt the procedure user.

Transitions to appendices are disruptive for the procedure user, who must abandon his location in the procedure, locate the appendix, read the appendix, and (if necessary) perform tasks as directed, and then return to his place in the procedure. This process is complicated by the fact that transitions to appendices are often implicit rather than explicit; in other words, rather than including an explicit cross-reference to the appendix, the procedure writer simply expects that the user will know to look in the appendix. Again, this simplifies the writer's job and complicates the user's job.

Excessive use of appendices is a danger sign. If a procedure includes appendices as high as AA or so (having already cycled once through the alphabet), something is probably wrong. Consider moving information from the appendices to the procedure, converting appendices to separate procedures, and so on. If it remains essential to use a great number of appendices, then provide help for the user in locating information in the appendices, in the form of explicit cross-references, indexes, and so on.

14.4   Include adequate identification information in procedures.

Summary

The cover page should include the procedure name and number, the procedure objective, and any necessary administrative information. The header or footer that appears on every page should include the procedure name and number, the page number, and any necessary administrative information.

Discussion

When a user picks up a procedure, he should know exactly what procedure it is, what the procedure applies to, and whether it is the current procedure. By including this information in the procedure, you are taking an important step towards ensuring that it is usable. This information appears on the cover page, the page header, or both.

Cover Page

The cover page is the first page of every procedure. The cover page identifies the procedure and should contain the following information:

- Obviously, the *procedure title* is an essential part of the title page. The title identifies the procedure. The title should be emphasized prominently; titles are typically bolded and surrounded by a good deal of white space. The title should be brief, but should adequately describe the procedure.

- The *procedure number* is also important. If procedure users typically identify procedures by number rather than title, then the number can be more important than the title and should be emphasized more heavily.

- An *objective* or *statement of scope* can also be useful. The objective is a short description of the procedure that supplements the title.

- The cover page should *identify the facility*. In large facilities, it may also be useful to identify the department or branch to which the procedure pertains.

- Finally, the cover page should include *administrative information*, such as review and approval signatures, the revision number, and the effective date of the procedure.

Page Header and Footer

The page header appears at the top of every page; the footer appears at the bottom of each page. The header or footer includes the identification information that must appear on every page:

- The *procedure title* and *number* should be repeated in the header or footer so that users can identify the procedure without referring to the cover page.

- In long procedures, it may be useful to repeat the *section title* in the header or footer.

- The *page number* must appear on every page. The page number should also include the total number of pages (e.g., *Page 7 of 32*) so that users are aware of the total number of pages in the procedure. This can be useful information, as the last page of a stapled procedure is sometimes separated from the procedure.

- Finally, the header should include adequate *administrative information*, such as the revision number or the effective date, so that users are certain they are working with the most current version of the procedure.

Part Four:
Writing Complex Steps

Chapter 15

Introduction: Writing Complex Steps

Part Two of this book discussed basic steps. While this discussion covered the fundamentals of step writing, it did not address the more complex types of steps that you frequently must write. Part Four turns to a discussion of these steps.

- Chapter 16 discusses lists, which are used to present a series of items (typically actions or conditions) in a step. Lists are frequently used in steps.

- Chapter 17 discusses conditional statements (which are also known as logic statements). Steps written as conditional statements contain actions that are taken only if a condition is met (e.g., *IF the ambient temperature is less that 45°F, THEN turn on the heater*).

- Chapter 18 discusses warnings (which warn of danger to workers), cautions (which warn of danger to machinery), and notes (which provide supplemental information).

- Chapter 19 discusses cross-references, which direct transitions in procedures (i.e., send users to another step).

- Chapter 20 discusses the special types of steps, including steps that are performed out of sequence, steps that verify that a given condition is met, steps that present equally acceptable alternatives, steps that assist users in diagnosing a situation, and steps that must be performed immediately in an emergency.

Chapter 16

Lists

A list is a sequence of items. This chapter presents one principle regarding lists.

16.1   Use lists to group and organize information.

Summary

Present a sequence of three or more items (e.g., actions, conditions) in a list format. Introduce the list with an overview. Provide a placekeeping aid for each item in the list.

Discussion

Lists "condense information into related groups that help readers to understand, organize, and remember information" (Mackh & Rew, 1991). Lists can present actions, conditions, criteria, equipment, and other types of information. This section will discuss the format for lists and the use of overviews to introduce lists.

The Format for Lists

Lists can be embedded into a step or emphasized with white space. Compare Figures 16.1 and 16.2. Figure 16.3 presents another example of a list.

The formatted list in Figure 16.2 is preferable when the list contains three or more items. According to Hartley (1982, p. 51), "Research suggests that readers prefer text which has lists or numbered sequences spaced out and separated, rather than run on in continuous text." Each item in the list is emphasized by being surrounded by white space so that readers can easily and efficiently scan through the list (Bensen, 1985). Each item has its own placekeeping aid, reducing the chance that an item will be overlooked. When a sequence of three or more items must be presented in a procedure, that sequence should be presented in a list.

[6]   Ensure that <u>all</u> of the following tests have been
             completed: SP-EG-105 series, SP-EG-100 series,
             and SP-EG-1 series.   ___

Figure 16.1. Embedded List. Compare this list with the list in Figure 16.2.

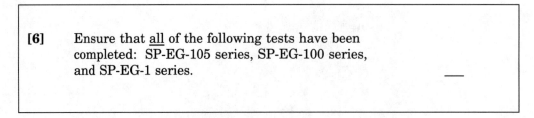

[6]   Ensure that <u>all</u> of the following tests have been
             completed:

             •   SP-EG-105 series   ___

             •   SP-EG-100 series   ___

             •   SP-EG-1 series   ___

Figure 16.2. White Space Used to Format a List. In this list, each listed item stands out
more clearly and has its own placekeeping aid.

[34]   Ensure that lights and switches are
             configured as follows:

             •   Primary Circuit Breaker - switch **on**   ___

             •   POWER ON 480 VAC - green light **on**   ___

             •   POWER ON 120 VAC - green light and
                    switch - **on**   ___

             •   Right door closed - amber light **on**   ___

Figure 16.3. Another Example of a List. Here, a list is used to present an equipment
configuration.

If a list contains only two items, then the use of white space to emphasize and
differentiate the items is optional. One important advantage of a formatted list is
that it allows a placekeeping aid for each item in the list; thus, if a list consists of
actions that require placekeeping aids, then the list format should be considered for
lists of even two items.

Overviews

It is important to provide a smooth transition into a list so that the user can deal effectively with the information presented (Mackh & Rew, 1991). This transition is created by the overview that introduces the list. In Figure 16.1, the overview is *Ensure that all of the following tests have been completed:*. The overview "sets the stage" for the list, alerting users to the type of information that is to follow.

Overviews are analogous to the topic sentences in a paragraph. A topic sentence is the first sentence of a paragraph; it should introduce the idea that will be developed in the paragraph. An overview does much the same thing, introducing the idea that will be developed in the list. Thus, much of the research on topic sentences can be applied to lists. The general conclusion in the research is that effective topic sentences are useful to readers. Lorch and Lorch (1985) found that topic sentences aid in recall. Kieras (1978) found that topic sentences (followed by "connected, coherent sentences" [p. 13]) minimized memory load. Spyridakis (1989a, 1989b; Spyridakis & Standal, 1987) also found that topic sentences were beneficial. By applying these findings, it can be assumed that effective overviews will aid in the comprehension and recall of listed items.

The overview should clearly indicate how many items in the list apply or should be performed. One possible approach for indicating this information is shown Figure 16.2, where the word all indicates that all tests must be performed. Similarly, the words any and one could be used to indicate that any test may be performed or that only one test should be performed. These words are underlined for emphasis, but they are not capitalized so that they do not detract from the emphasis of conditional terms. The overview should also end with a colon, so that it is apparent that the overview is related to the list that follows.

Chapter 17

Conditional Statements

Many steps unconditionally direct users to perform an action or a set of actions. In some instances, however, procedure writers must place restrictions on particular steps and direct users to perform an action only if a specific condition is met. In such cases, the step must clearly specify the condition to be met and must identify the relationship between that condition and the action to be taken. Steps that include a condition and an action are called conditional statements. In procedures, all conditional statements should be written according to formal rules of logic; therefore, these conditional statements are often called logic statements. This chapter discusses why conditional statements should be used in procedures and how to use conditional statements properly. It presents these principles:

- Use conditional statements to present conditional information in procedures.

- Use conditional terms accurately, appropriately, and consistently.

- Use the conditional terms <u>AND</u> or <u>OR</u> separately to combine conditions when necessary, but avoid complex sequences of conditional terms.

17.1 Use conditional statements to present conditional information in procedures.

Summary

Conditional statements should always be used to present conditional information in procedures. These statements describe a condition first and then describe the action to be taken if that condition is met. These statements use the conditional terms <u>IF</u> or <u>WHEN</u> to present the condition, <u>THEN</u> to present the action, and <u>NOT</u> to negate conditions. These terms should be consistently emphasized throughout procedures.

Discussion

Steps that consist of conditions and actions tend to be long and complex. In addition, different writers may convey the same conditional information in different ways. For example, a simple conditional statement can be written several ways, as shown in Figure 17.1.

If the pretrip alarm for LO SG PRESS CH PRE-TRIP actuates, direct the secondary operator to lower the automatic steam generator-low setpoint.

Direct the secondary operator to lower the automatic steam generator-low setpoint if the pretrip alarm for LO SG PRESS CH PRE-TRIP actuates.

Direct the secondary operator to lower the automatic steam generator-low setpoint, but only if the pretrip alarm for LO SG PRESS CH PRE-TRIP actuates.

Do not direct the secondary operator to lower the automatic steam generator-low setpoint unless the pretrip alarm for LO SG PRESS CH PRE-TRIP actuates.

The secondary operator shall be directed to lower the automatic steam generator-low setpoint if the pretrip alarm for LO SG PRESS CH PRE-TRIP actuates.

Figure 17.1. Different Ways of Writing the Same Step. Without the consistent use of conditional statements described in this chapter, a step could be written several different ways.

In order to decrease the complexity of conditional statements and make them more consistent, conditional statements should be written according to the rules of formal logic. Conditional terms are the specific words that indicate conditions and the subsequent actions to take when certain conditions exist. The conditional terms commonly used in procedures are <u>IF</u>, <u>WHEN</u>, <u>THEN</u>, <u>AND</u>, <u>OR</u>, and <u>NOT</u>. These terms derive from Boolean logic. George Boole (1815-1864) was an English mathematician and logician who devised this system of formal logic. There are many books devoted to discussions of formal logic, such as *Formal Logic: Its Scope and Limitations* by Jeffrey (1967), but for this discussion you need only remember that conditional terms are used according to specific rules of logic.

If these conditional statements were rewritten according to the rules of formal logic, the various statements in Figure 17.1 would all look something like this:

IF the pretrip alarm for LO SG PRESS CH PRE-TRIP actuates,
THEN direct the secondary operator to lower the automatic steam
generator-low setpoint.

Writing conditional statements according to the rules of logic increases their consistency; there is only one way to construct a given conditional statement according to the rules of logic. Also, using a formal, structured approach to writing conditional statements decreases the likelihood that the statement will be misunderstood. The reader can apply the same rules when interpreting the step as the writer used when writing the step. Thus, it becomes easier for users to understand conditional information that is presented in conditional statements.

The most important rule to remember about conditional statements is that the condition always goes *before* the action. If the action comes first, the user is likely to perform the action regardless of whether the condition has been met. Here the action precedes the condition:

Direct the secondary operator to lower
the automatic steam generator-low setpoint
IF the pretrip alarm for LO SG PRESS CH PRE-TRIP actuates.

If a user were to encounter this procedure step, he or she could direct the secondary operator to lower the automatic steam generator set point without realizing that the steam generator set point should only be lowered when a specific condition exists; that is, only if the pretrip alarm for LO SG PRESS CH PRE-TRIP actuates. Because carrying out an action at an inappropriate time may have serious consequences, *always* write the condition before the action in a conditional statement so that the user encounters the condition first.

IF the pretrip alarm for LO SG PRESS CH PRE-TRIP actuates,
THEN direct the secondary operator to lower the automatic steam
generator-low setpoint.

Conditional terms should always be emphasized in procedures. As discussed in Section 13.1, emphasis on conditional terms actually serves more of a coding function. Typically the nuclear power industry uses capitalization and underlining to emphasize conditional terms. Therefore, throughout this chapter you will notice that the terms IF, WHEN, THEN, AND, OR, IF NOT, and NOT are capitalized and underlined so that they stand out from other words in the text. Other emphasis techniques, such as those discussed in Chapter 13, could be used to emphasize these terms, but capitalization and underlining were chosen here as an example of one effective technique.

Regardless of which emphasis technique is chosen to make conditional terms stand out, the emphasis technique for conditional terms must be used *only* for conditional terms, not for other words in a procedure as well. For example, if conditional terms are capitalized and underlined and occasionally other non-conditional term words are also capitalized and underlined, the conditional terms are no longer unique. A user could no longer look at a capitalized, underlined word in the procedure and identify it as quickly as a conditional term. Emphasizing conditional terms clearly divides the conditional statement into conditions and actions. Figure 17.2 demonstrates this effect. At a glance, the user can not only recognize a conditional statement, but can also quickly distinguish the various parts of the conditional statement. Dividing conditional statements into conditions and actions so that the user can readily identify the discrete parts of the statement becomes even more critical as conditional statements become more complex.

If the status light is green, then push the override button.

IF the status light is green, THEN push the override button.

Figure 17.2. Use of Emphasis in Conditional Statements. Here, capitalization and underlining make conditional terms, conditions, and action stand out.

The use of white space can also add emphasis in conditional statements. By always having the conditional terms IF, WHEN, and THEN start new lines, the white space created by the line break adds emphasis and helps the user distinguish between the conditions and the actions in the conditional statement (Barfield, 1986; Hartley, 1982; Stevens, 1981).

IF the status light is green,
THEN push the override button.

Here the user can clearly see the condition (*IF the status light is green,*) and the action (*THEN push the override button*) by virtue of the line break between the condition and the action. More information on the use of white space is presented in Section 11.2.

You must also check conditional statements to ensure that the statements are clear and logically correct. In other words, the conditional statement must cover every eventuality for a particular condition and action. As you write a procedure, you should walk through the logic of all conditional statements (or a series of conditional statements), step by step. You must ensure that conditional statements make sense and clearly direct users to take appropriate actions.

17.2   Use conditional terms accurately, appropriately, and consistently.

Summary

Each conditional term in a procedure has a specific meaning and a specific use. The conditional term IF signifies a condition that may or may not happen. WHEN signifies a condition that is very likely to occur. All steps containing IF and WHEN should also include the conditional term THEN. THEN signifies the action that should be taken if a condition is met. THEN should not be used to combine actions or items. The conditional term <u>NOT</u> is used to clearly distinguish a negated condition. Whenever possible, however, writers should phrase conditional information positively. Do not use <u>NOT</u> if another word can convey information more clearly. Finally, use the phrase <u>IF</u> <u>NOT</u> to express action to take if a condition is not met.

Discussion

This section individually discusses the conditional terms used in procedures.

Using <u>IF</u>

Webster's New Collegiate Dictionary (1977) states that *if* means "in the event that." Therefore, the conditional term <u>IF</u> might be interpreted to mean "in the event that this condition has been met, take the following action." The procedure user understands that there is the likelihood that a condition beginning with <u>IF</u> will not be met in the course of performing a procedure.

Use <u>IF</u> consistently. <u>IF</u> should be used to introduce conditions (1) that may exist and (2) that determine whether the following action or actions should be performed. <u>IF</u> should only be used at the beginning of conditional statements; <u>IF</u> should not be hidden inside action steps. Figure 17.3 illustrates why <u>IF</u> should not be hidden inside action steps.

Establish cooling water to secondary systems <u>IF</u> any non-vital 4.16 kv buses are energized.

<u>IF</u> any non-vital 4.16 kv buses are energized,
<u>THEN</u> establish cooling water to secondary systems.

Figure 17.3. Hidden Condition. The first sentence illustrates an <u>IF</u> hidden within an action step. The user is likely to perform the action first and then read the statement, only to discover that perhaps the action should not have been performed. The second sentence illustrates the correct use of <u>IF</u>.

Using <u>WHEN</u>

<u>WHEN</u> introduces a condition that is expected to occur sometime during the execution of the procedure, as shown in Figure 17.4.

> **[3]**   <u>WHEN</u> at least 3 class inverters are energized,
> <u>THEN</u> reset <u>all</u> of the following:
>
> - SIAS   —
>
> - CSAS   —
>
> - RAS   —

Figure 17.4. Conditional Statement Using <u>WHEN</u>. <u>WHEN</u> is used to introduce conditions that are expected to occur.

In the above example, at least three class inverters are expected to be energized at some point during the procedure. When that happens, the user knows it is then time to reset the SIAS, CSAS, and RAS.

<u>WHEN</u> can actually have two related meanings. One meaning is that the user must stop and wait until the condition is met before continuing on with the action. The other meaning is that the user can expect the condition to occur, but the user does not have to wait for the condition to occur before continuing on with the procedure. It is important to give the user guidance about how to interpret <u>WHEN</u> in a procedure by including the phrase *Continue in this procedure* (or a similar phrase) in steps where the user can go on in the procedure while waiting for the condition to be met (see Figure 17.5).

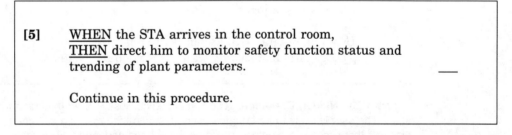

> **[5]**   <u>WHEN</u> the STA arrives in the control room,
> <u>THEN</u> direct him to monitor safety function status and
> trending of plant parameters.   —
>
> Continue in this procedure.

Figure 17.5.   Instructions to Continue. Here, users continue in the procedure if the STA (Shift Technical Advisor) has not arrived in the control room. They take the action when he arrives.

Note that the instructions to *Continue in this procedure* are separated from the conditional statement by one blank line. This white space emphasizes the instruction and helps ensure that the user will not overlook it.

You must use *Continue in this procedure* carefully because you are requiring the user to remember this step as he or she continues on to subsequent steps. When the phrase *Continue in this procedure* is appended to the conditional statement, the step becomes a *concurrent* step. Although they are essential at times, concurrent steps should be used sparingly because they require users to remember information. You should remind the user to perform the concurrent step on subsequent pages of the procedure. This reminder should appear in a consistent location (e.g., on the facing page) and should be emphasized so that it stands out. Section 20.1 discusses concurrent steps in greater detail.

As with IF, WHEN should only be used at the beginning of a conditional statement; WHEN should not be hidden inside action steps.

Using THEN

All steps containing IF and WHEN should also include THEN. This convention promotes consistency and uniquely distinguishes conditional statements from other kinds of steps. This convention also assures you that every conditional statement has an associated action and that the action is consistently identified.

> IF the level for any steam generator is less than 0% wr,
> THEN restore the level.

THEN should not be used to combine non-conditional items or to make run-on sentences. An incorrect use of THEN is *Place the mechanism into the bin, THEN close the lid*. In this case, there is no conditional information in the sentence. There are only two actions connected by THEN. Use of THEN in this situation is liable to be confusing.

Using NOT

The conditional term NOT is used to distinguish a negated condition.

> IF the diesel generator is NOT running,
> THEN direct the primary operator to manually start the diesel generator.

NOT is emphasized with capitalization and underlining to make sure that users do not misunderstand and read the condition as a positive statement. As a general rule of thumb, use NOT in place of a negating prefix such as *in-* or *un-* to negate a condition. For example, rather than say, *IF the demineralized water system is inadequate,* you should say, *IF the demineralized water system is NOT adequate.* The rationale for using NOT in this situation is that it clearly indicates that the condition is negated; *inadequate*, on the other hand, could be misread as *adequate*.

However, you should minimize the use of NOT because readers must often read and reread a negative statement to understand its meaning. Positively phrased sentences are usually easier to understand and less prone to misinterpretation (Wason, 1959, 1961). Therefore, whenever possible, phrase conditions positively. When one word that does not begin with *in-* or *un-* can denote the negative state (such as saying *IF the valve is closed* instead of saying *IF the valve is NOT open*) you should use the one word instead of NOT to negate the condition. Section 5.5 discusses the presentation of negative information in more detail.

Using **IF** **NOT**

So far this section has discussed how to write simple conditional statements that direct a user to take an action when a condition is met. When you must write a conditional statement that directs a user to take action when a condition is *not* met, you should use the conditional term **IF** NOT. The term **IF** NOT allows you to express two actions that depend on the same condition: one action is performed if the condition *is* met and the other is performed if the condition *is not* met (see Figure 17.6).

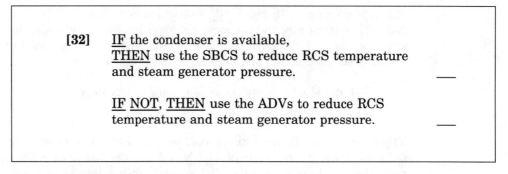

> [32] **IF** the condenser is available,
>   **THEN** use the SBCS to reduce RCS temperature
>   and steam generator pressure.   ___
>
>   **IF** NOT, **THEN** use the ADVs to reduce RCS
>   temperature and steam generator pressure.   ___

Figure 17.6. Use of IF NOT. IF NOT expresses a contingent action that is taken if the condition is not met.

In this example, if the condition of having a condenser available is not met, the user understands that he or she must use the ADVs to reduce RCS temperature and steam generator pressure.

Although **IF** NOT is useful for writing some conditional statements, it should be used only for simple statements that contain one condition and one action. Using **IF** NOT after multiple conditions or multiple actions may cause a user to misinterpret the conditional statement and make an error. For example, the term **IF** NOT should not have been used in Figure 17.7.

> [7] **IF** the power for the trickle head system is off,
>   **THEN** perform the following:
>
>   •   Plug in the 120 V ac power.   ___
>
>   •   Record the date and time at
>   which power was applied.   ___
>
>   **IF** NOT, **THEN** energize main busses.   ___

Figure 17.7. Incorrect Use of IF NOT. IF NOT should not be used in conditional statements containing multiple actions.

Given this conditional statement, the user might ask, "<u>IF</u> <u>NOT</u> what?" It is not immediately clear that the <u>IF</u> <u>NOT</u> in this step applies to the trickle head system being off. Literally, the step is saying, *IF the trickle head system is <u>NOT</u> off,* but you can see how a user might become confused and make an error in executing this step. The term <u>IF</u> <u>NOT</u> should not have been used here because two listed actions separate the <u>IF</u> <u>NOT</u> action from the condition and require the user to not only remember the original condition but also to interpret the double negative *not off*. A clearer way to convey this information would be to dispense with <u>IF</u> <u>NOT</u> altogether and write two steps, as shown in Figure 17.8.

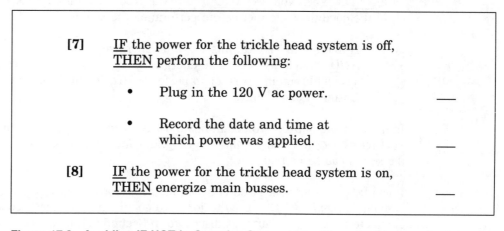

[7]   <u>IF</u> the power for the trickle head system is off,
<u>THEN</u> perform the following:

-    Plug in the 120 V ac power.   —

-    Record the date and time at
  which power was applied.   —

[8]   <u>IF</u> the power for the trickle head system is on,
<u>THEN</u> energize main busses.   —

Figure 17.8. Avoiding <u>IF</u> <u>NOT</u> in Complex Steps. Here, Figure 17.7 is corrected by breaking it into two steps.

Remember that <u>IF</u> <u>NOT</u> is best used only for simple conditional statements. If multiple actions separate the <u>IF</u> <u>NOT</u> action from the original condition, or if the <u>IF</u> <u>NOT</u> action requires the user to interpret a double negative based on the original condition, users may easily become confused and make an error in executing the step.

17.3 Use the conditional terms <u>AND</u> or <u>OR</u> separately to combine conditions when necessary, but avoid complex sequences of conditional terms.

Summary

<u>AND</u> and <u>OR</u> combine conditions. <u>AND</u> indicates that all conditions must be met before action is taken. Usually the conditional term <u>OR</u> is inclusive in procedures and is used to combine conditions for statements in which one or more than one condition must be met before an associated action can be carried out. Writers should maintain the distinction between <u>AND</u> and *and* as well as the distinction between <u>OR</u> and *or*. Finally, to keep conditional statements from becoming too long and complex, avoid using <u>AND</u> and <u>OR</u> in the same conditional statement.

Discussion

This section discusses the difference between the conditional terms <u>AND</u> and <u>OR</u>. The section also discusses when each of these terms is appropriate to use in conditional statements.

Using <u>AND</u>

If you want to combine conditions in a conditional statement to indicate that *all* of the conditions must be met before the associated action can be carried out, use the term <u>AND</u>. When you use <u>AND</u> in this way you are telling the user to ensure that all of the conditions are met before performing the action.

> <u>IF</u> both 4.16 kv vital buses are de-energized
> <u>AND</u> the 525 kv grid is de-energized,
> <u>THEN</u> direct an operator to perform Attachment 2 of this procedure,
> Battery Load Control.

In the example above, two conditions must be checked: the status of the 4.16 kv vital buses and the status of the 525 kv grid. *Both* conditions must be met before the action can be carried out.

It can be useful to distinguish between the conditional term <u>AND</u> and the conjunction *and*. <u>AND</u> is used to join two conditions when each condition is a complete clause. (A clause, as discussed in Section 5.1, contains a subject, verb, and object.) In all other instances, *and* is a conjunction. Figure 17.9 demonstrates the correct use of <u>AND</u>.

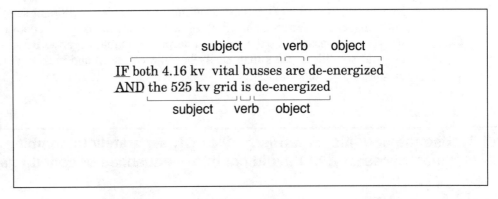

Figure 17.9. Use of <u>AND</u> to Join Complete Clauses. The two conditions joined by <u>AND</u> are complete clauses, meaning that each contains a subject, verb, and object.

Now consider the following example, which fails to use <u>AND</u> according to this rule:

> <u>IF</u> a safety injection has actuated
> <u>AND</u> pressurizer pressure is greater than 300 psia
> <u>AND</u> stable,
> <u>THEN</u> stop <u>all</u> operating HPSI and CS pumps.

Here, the third "condition" is not a complete clause—it is simply the word *stable*. Hence, it should be introduced by the conjunction *and*:

> <u>IF</u> a safety injection has actuated
> <u>AND</u> pressurizer pressure is greater than 300 psia and stable,
> <u>THEN</u> stop <u>all</u> operating HPSI and CS pumps.

Figure 17.10 shows how the second condition is now a complete clause.

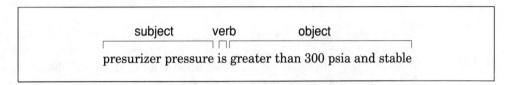

Figure 17.10. Use of *and* in a Compound Object. This condition is one complete clause. Confusion may arise because the clause includes *and*, but *and* is used in a compound object—it does not join two complete clauses.

There are two advantages to distinguishing between <u>AND</u> and *and*. The first is that if *and* is always capitalized and underlined, then the procedure will quickly become cluttered with <u>AND</u>s (and <u>OR</u>s, if they are treated the same way). Fully capitalizing and underlining <u>AND</u> will detract from effective true emphasis (due to overuse) and from effective coding, because <u>AND</u> no longer consistently signals the beginning of a condition.

The second advantage to distinguishing between <u>AND</u> and *and* is that failure to do so fragments information that should be grouped. Consider this example again:

> <u>IF</u> a safety injection has actuated
> <u>AND</u> pressurizer pressure is greater than 300 psia
> <u>AND</u> stable,
> <u>THEN</u> stop <u>all</u> operating HPSI and CS pumps.

Use of <u>AND</u> separates *pressurizer pressure is greater than 300 psia* from *stable*, when these words belong together. In other words, the example above makes it look like the user is checking three things, when in fact he is checking only two—(1) the status of safety injection and (2) pressurizer pressure. When the procedure writer distinguishes between <u>AND</u> and *and*, the step clearly conveys this information.

Finally, whenever you have three or more conditions, use a list format rather than multiple <u>AND</u>s. A user can more clearly identify a list as a group of related items (NRC, 1982). Lists are discussed further in Section 16.1.

Using <u>OR</u>

The conditional term <u>OR</u> is used in conditional statements when only one condition must be met before the associated action can be carried out.

IF Reactor Power Cutback System Trouble,
window 4A11A, is lit
OR the AUTO ACTUATE OUT OF SERVICE
light is NOT lit,
THEN GO TO Reactor Power Cutback,
41OP-1SF04.

In this case, two conditions must be checked: the status of the Reactor Power Cutback System Trouble, window 4A11A, and the AUTO ACTUATE OUT OF SERVICE light. If either condition is met, the action should be carried out.

As with AND and *and*, there is a distinction between the conditional term OR and the conjunction *or*. OR is used only in conditional statements according to the rules of logic. Because OR is a conditional term, it should always be emphasized. The conjunction *or* should not be emphasized.

Also, keep in mind the difference between an inclusive and an exclusive OR. An inclusive OR means that an action can be carried out when one or more than one condition is met. If there are two conditions combined with an inclusive OR, it does not matter whether one or both of the conditions are met. As long as at least one condition is met, the action can be carried out. On the other hand, an exclusive OR means that either one condition or the other, but not both, must be met. An exclusive OR excludes the possibility that more than one condition can be met before an action is carried out. Figure 17.11 illustrates that distinction.

First Condition	Second Condition	Inclusive OR	Exclusive OR
true	true	take action	do not take action
true	false	take action	take action
false	true	take action	take action
false	false	do not take action	do not take action

Figure 17.11. The Distinction Between Inclusive OR and Exclusive OR. This truth table illustrates the difference between the two forms of OR.

Ordinarily, we can distinguish between inclusive OR and exclusive OR by the context in which they appear. For example, when a waiter asks, "Would you like something to drink or an appetizer?" you know that you could have a drink or an appetizer or both. The inclusive OR is being used in this case. But when the waiter asks, "Would you like a baked potato or rice?" then you know an exclusive OR is being used. In this case the waiter is saying that you may have a potato, or rice, but not both. However, we do not want procedure users to rely on context to interpret OR in the operation of complex technological systems. Because you will rarely (if ever) have reason to use the exclusive OR to join two conditions, we recommend that you only use inclusive OR in procedure conditional statements. In other words, a conditional statement using OR in a procedure should always mean that one or more than one condition must be met in order for the associated action to be carried out. Consistent use of <u>OR</u> will eliminate confusion and reliance on context.

Finally, whenever you have three or more contingencies, use a list format rather than multiple <u>OR</u>s. A user can more clearly identify a list as a group of related items (NRC, 1982). Lists are discussed further in Section 16.1.

Combining <u>AND</u> and <u>OR</u>

Conditional statements can be difficult to interpret if they are long and complex. In order to keep conditional statements short and simple, break a long, complicated step into more than one logic statement if necessary. A series of short, unambiguous conditional statements is better than one long, complex, difficult-to-understand conditional statement.

In particular, avoid using <u>AND</u> and <u>OR</u> in the same conditional statement. When <u>AND</u> and <u>OR</u> appear together in the same statement, the user may interpret the statement in two different ways. The conditional statement below illustrates this point. The context is that you are driving to the store and must decide whether to put the top of your convertible down.

> <u>IF</u> it is a beautiful day,
> <u>AND</u> you want to impress your neighbors,
> <u>OR</u> the car needs airing,
> <u>THEN</u> put the car top down.

Borrowing a technique from algebra, we can use parentheses to indicate the two ways to read this statement:

> <u>IF</u> (it is a beautiful day <u>AND</u> you want to impress your neighbors),
> <u>OR</u> the car needs airing,
> <u>THEN</u> put the car top down.

> <u>IF</u> it is a beautiful day
> <u>AND</u> (you want to impress your neighbors <u>OR</u> the car needs airing)
> <u>THEN</u> put the car top down.

This complex conditional statement is ambiguous. The user might wonder, "Should I put the top down on a cloudy day?" Using the first interpretation, the answer would be yes, if the car needs airing, put the top down regardless of the weather. However, using the second interpretation, the answer is no because it must be a beautiful day in order to put the car top down. In the above example, the consequences of choosing the wrong interpretation may not be very serious—at worst the user might get wet if the cloudy weather turns to rain. However, in many industrial settings a misinterpretation could have very serious consequences.

To avoid writing ambiguous or confusing conditional statements, break complex conditional statements into several simple conditional statements. Assuming the second interpretation is correct, the previous example might be broken into the following simple conditional statements:

[1]   <u>IF</u> it is a beautiful day
<u>AND</u> you want to impress your neighbors
<u>THEN</u> put the car top down and GO TO Step 3.

[2]   <u>IF</u> it is a beautiful day
<u>AND</u> your car needs airing,
<u>THEN</u> put the car top down.

[3]   Drive to the store.

The reference to *GO TO Step [3]* is necessary because if it is a beautiful day and you are driving your car, there is no need to perform Step **[2]**—you already have the top down.

These two simple statements clearly tell the user what actions to take. Based on this information, the user cannot give a wrong answer to the question, "Should I put the top down on a cloudy day?" because in each case the condition that it be a beautiful day must be met. In addition, by seeing the long, complex conditional statement broken into two simpler statements, the user realizes that he or she need not read the second conditional statement if the conditions of the first statement are met. Figure 17.12 illustrates that both statements lead to the same end point, but the user need only take one of the conditional statement paths to get to that end point.

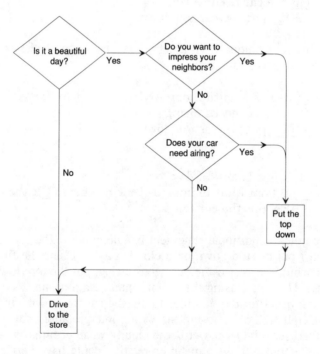

Figure 17.12 Flowchart Version of a Set of Conditional Steps. This flowchart illustrates that two separate conditional statements can lead to the same end point. The user need only follow one of the conditional statements to the end point.

The inclusion of the instructions to *GO TO Step [3]* points out an important fact—you must walk through the logic of the procedure, trying *all* permutations of conditions, to determine that your steps make sense. This can be a complex and subtle process but it is very important.

Chapter 18

Warnings, Cautions, and Notes

Warnings alert users to potential hazards that may result in death or injury to workers or the public. Cautions alert users to potential hazards that may damage machinery or equipment. Notes call attention to important supplemental information that may enhance a user's understanding and performance of the procedure.

This chapter presents six principles for writing warnings, cautions, and notes:

- Include warnings and cautions in procedures.

- Ensure that actions do not appear in warnings and cautions.

- Warnings and cautions must identify a single hazard, the consequences of the hazard, and any critical time constraints.

- Present warnings and cautions in a unique format.

- Place warnings and cautions on the same page as and immediately before the step to which they apply.

- Use notes to present supplemental information.

18.1 Include warnings and cautions in procedures.

Summary

Inadequate or missing warnings and cautions may result in injury or even death. Warnings and cautions are important because users understand operations but may not know the hazards associated with those operations. Also, we typically do not perceive or estimate risk accurately.

Discussion

Warnings and cautions are the most critical type of supporting information in procedures. Because procedure users may deal directly with hazardous equipment, work in hazardous situations, or take actions that affect the safety of others, they must be informed of any dangers involved in these activities. This information is provided in warnings and cautions. Inadequate warnings and cautions may result in injury or death. It is your responsibility as a procedure writer to include proper warnings and cautions in procedures.

Don't assume that procedure users will know to avoid dangerous situations. Although users may have enough knowledge to operate a system, their knowledge may not include adequate awareness of the hazards involved in system operation. Further, empirical research has demonstrated that people typically do not estimate or perceive risk accurately. When individuals are asked to make judgments about risk-related events, they typically underestimate the risk for events in which they lack actual personal experience and overestimate the risk for events that receive much media attention (Slovic, Fischhoff, & Lichtenstein, 1982). Also, when making judgments about risk, individuals often use rules of thumb (heuristics) that result in their excluding important available information about risk (Payne, 1976). Even when people are very familiar with a task, they can underestimate the risk associated with the task. In fact, people are likely to minimize the risk of carrying out a very familiar task. It is, therefore, inappropriate and possibly dangerous to rely on the user to know or to figure out the potential risks in operating a system. Proper warnings and cautions must be included in procedures.

You as the procedure writer cannot include proper warnings and cautions in a procedure without a complete understanding of the potential hazards inherent in the tasks, systems, and processes covered by the procedure. Therefore, you (or another appropriate person) must perform an exhaustive investigation to identify all of the potential hazards for each procedure step. Input for this investigation should come from procedure users, technical specialists, subject matter experts (including operations), and all available documentation (including drawings, descriptions, technical specifications, safety documents, administrative documents, accident reports, and so on).

18.2   Ensure that actions do not appear in warnings and cautions.

Summary

Including actions in warnings and cautions may confuse users. Actions in warnings and cautions may also increase the likelihood that a user will overlook an action. Finally, to ensure that you do not "hide" an action in a warning or caution, use the active voice, negative imperative mood for warnings and cautions.

Discussion

One of the most difficult aspects of writing effective warnings and cautions is writing them so that they do not include actions that belong in steps instead. The main reason we do not include actions in warnings or cautions is so that actions are not overlooked. Further, steps offer a better format for presenting actions. Steps include placekeeping aids and step numbers to help users track their place in the procedure.

Why Actions Do Not Belong in Cautions

The example below shows an incorrect caution that includes an action.

CAUTION

<u>WHEN</u> dc voltage has increased to at least 100 V dc, <u>THEN</u> close the input breaker. Closing the input breaker sooner may cause a power surge on the inverter.

Users reading the caution in the above example might not register the information as an action. When users see a caution they expect to see supplementary information, not instructional information. Therefore, actions presented in warnings and cautions may confuse users and may increase the possibility of users making errors (Fuchs, Engelschall, & Imlay, 1981).

The action should be presented in a step. If the user must be alerted to a potential hazard associated with performing that step, the information on the potential hazard should be written as an active voice, negative imperative statement *above* the step. Figure 18.1 shows the corrected caution and step.

CAUTION

Do not close the input breaker until dc voltage has increased to at least 100 V dc; otherwise a power surge on the inverter may occur.

---

[3]   <u>WHEN</u> dc voltage has increased to at least 100 V dc,
         <u>THEN</u> close the input breaker.   ___

Figure 18.1. Integration of a Caution and a Step. Here, the action is presented in a step while the cautionary information related to the step is presented in the caution before the step.

Although the caution in the example above is written as an imperative, it is not an action. It instructs the user *not* to do something; in other words, it instructs the user to leave things the way they are—to leave the breaker open. Hence, it is a negative imperative. The step below the caution provides explicit instructions on when to close the input breaker during the procedure. The caution was not the place to tell the user about the action. Thus, a step was added to tell the user when to close the input breaker.

Although Section 5.5 stated that negative statements are often more difficult to understand, warnings and cautions often justify the use of negative statements. Be careful, however, to avoid using double negatives, such as *Do not leave the valve unlocked*, and other convoluted negative constructions in warnings and cautions. The alternative phrasing, *Lock the valve*, is much easier to understand. Further, being able to rewrite the negative statement *Do not leave the valve unlocked* as the positive statement *Lock the valve* indicates that it may be an action belonging in a step format rather than in a caution.

Using the Passive Voice

Often, writers try using the passive voice to "hide" an action in a warning or caution. For example, a writer may try to eliminate any hint of an action by writing:

****

WARNING

Bus bars and circuit boards inside the battery charger access doors may be energized, presenting an electrocution hazard.
****

The warning above is written in the passive voice, as evidenced by the verb phrase *may be energized*. In this particular warning, the object is omitted—the bus bars and circuit boards may be energized, but by *what?* As you may remember from Section 5.4, objects are often omitted from passive sentences if the object is unimportant. Here, the bus bars and circuit boards are energized by the cables that run to them; because this information is not important, the procedure writer omitted it.

But, because the object is omitted from this sentence, the user reading the procedure is left to fill in the missing information. A user could assume that the object was *you* (i.e., himself or herself) and could interpret the caution as an instruction to energize the bus bars and circuit boards—*You may energize the bus bars and circuit boards.*

The example below addresses the potential for this type of error by explicitly wording the warning as an instruction not to touch the bus bars or circuit boards.

****

WARNING

Do not touch the bus bars and circuit boards inside the battery charger access doors because they may be energized, presenting an electrocution hazard.
****

Again, we have returned to the negative imperative as the best form for presenting this type of information in a warning or caution. The previous example points out the dangers of using the passive voice in a warning (or anywhere). Although there will be instances when the passive voice is the best way of presenting information, there are other situations where it can get you into trouble. Thus, you should avoid the temptation to use the passive voice to hide an action in a warning or caution because you may introduce the potential for user error and confusion.

Further, if a writer casts an action as a passive sentence in a caution, the action is still there, it is just more difficult to see because it's implied. So, in addition to still presenting an action, the caution is confusing. By using the passive voice, the writer has not solved anything. He has just made the caution more difficult to understand. Look at the two cautions below.

CAUTION

Temperature must be maintained above 185°F or the solution will gel.

CAUTION

Maintain temperature above 185°F or the solution will gel.

The writer of the first caution used the passive voice and in doing so mistook a passively phrased action for cautionary information. In reality, this caution does not warn the user of any potential hazard. Instead it directs the user to take action. Rewriting the caution in the active voice, as shown in the second example, allows the writer to clearly see that the caution is really an action step and therefore should be presented in a step.

18.3   Warnings and cautions must identify a single hazard, the consequences of the hazard, and any critical time constraints.

Summary

Complete warnings and cautions identify (1) the hazard, (2) the consequences of the hazard, and (3) any critical time constraints associated with the hazard. Ensure that each warning, caution, and note deals with only one topic.

Discussion

The best way to avoid something is to know exactly what you are trying to avoid. Unless sufficient information is provided in a warning or caution, the procedure user may not understand and appreciate the risk related to a potential hazard. At a minimum, each warning and caution must identify the hazard and the consequences of the hazard. Time considerations may also be critical for some hazards. In such cases, the warnings or cautions for those hazards must state important time considerations (Ballard & Rode-Perkins, 1987). Harris and Wiklund (1989) suggest that more threatening warnings and cautions are perceived more effectively. Therefore, do not minimize a potential hazard when writing warnings and cautions. If, for example, death from electrocution is a potential consequence, the warning should explicitly state that the user may die if the warning is not followed. The warning below exemplifies a complete warning.

****

WARNING

Charging or discharging batteries generates hydrogen gas. Do not smoke, use open flames, or create arcs or sparks in the vicinity of batteries because an explosion may occur.
****

Notice how information is arranged in the above warning. The warning identifies the potential hazard first: *Charging or discharging batteries generates hydrogen gas*. Then the warning presents an imperative instruction telling the user what not to do, followed by a short description of the consequence. The directive *Do not smoke, use open flames, or create arcs or sparks in the vicinity of batteries because an explosion may occur* is an example of the active voice, negative imperative mood in warnings and cautions. Also, make sure that the action steps below warnings and cautions are clear and concise. Avoid using unnecessary verbiage in the steps that may make the intent of the warning or caution more difficult to recognize or understand.

Finally, each warning and caution must address only one topic. Presenting only one topic in a warning or caution helps the user understand the intent of the warning or caution better and assists the user in recalling or checking the cautionary information presented in a step. The example below illustrates how confusing warnings and cautions become if more than one topic is addressed.

****

WARNING

Battery electrolyte contains sulfuric acid and will cause burning if it comes in contact with skin or eyes. Do not wear loose clothing near moving equipment.

****

Given this warning, the user would not quickly understand which potential hazard was more immediate or what steps to take to avoid the hazard. This warning should be rewritten into two separate warnings: one addressing the hazard of battery electrolytes coming in contact with the skin or eyes and the other addressing the hazard of wearing loose clothing near moving equipment.

18.4 Present warnings and cautions in a unique format.

Summary

Warnings and cautions should be formatted to draw attention to their critical nature. Clearly differentiating warnings and cautions from the rest of the procedure reduces the effort required to determine the purpose of the warning or caution. Also, consider the user's expectations when deciding whether to consistently call potential hazards involving personnel or equipment only cautions or only warnings. Ask yourself whether the user would expect you to distinguish between the two types of hazards.

Discussion

This section discusses the use of a unique format for warnings and cautions. The section also discusses why a writer must adhere to user expectations when deciding whether to use the terms warning or caution for information on hazards.

Use a Unique Format

Warnings and cautions in a procedure must be uniquely emphasized to draw attention to their critical nature (Ballard & Rode-Perkins, 1987). (Section 13.1 discusses emphasis techniques.) Some evidence (McCarthy et al., 1984) suggests that people do not pay much attention to warnings. For example, people generally do not read warning labels on products or pay attention to a flight attendant's preflight briefing in commercial air travel. One way to draw the user's attention to warnings and cautions is to present them in a unique format. Using a unique emphasis technique to clearly differentiate warnings and cautions from other parts of the procedure will help users recognize the critical nature of warnings and cautions. If users know what kind of information to expect when they see a specific format, they can more easily and quickly process the information presented.

Simple ways to emphasize warnings and cautions include centering, bolding, or underlining the word *warning* or *caution*. Such emphasis will help users to quickly and easily recognize that cautionary information is being presented. Another formatting technique that can emphasize warnings and cautions is to use white space to separate the warning or caution from the flow of action steps in the procedure. Section 11.2 presents more information about the use of white space as an emphasis technique. Boxing around a warning or caution can also be used as a means of separation. The examples below illustrate how emphasis techniques can be used effectively to differentiate between warnings and cautions.

CAUTION

Do not run the engine more than 6 hrs continuously as it may overheat.

****
WARNING

Do not smoke near gasoline fumes because it may cause an explosion.
****

In the above example, the caution is differentiated from regular text by being centered within a box with the word *caution* presented in all capital bold letters. A slightly different emphasis technique is used for the warning: it is centered between two lines of asterisks and the word *warning* appears in all capital letters.

The Distinction Between Warnings and Cautions

So far this discussion has made a distinction between warnings, which describe hazards to people, and cautions, which discuss hazards to equipment. However, some facilities may choose not to differentiate between warnings and cautions. In some procedures only the term *caution* or the term *warning* may be used to alert users to both personnel and equipment hazards.

Always present information about hazards in accordance with the users' expectations. At some facilities users expect procedures to differentiate between hazards to people (i.e., warnings) and hazards to equipment (i.e., cautions). Users at other facilities, however, may expect the term *warning* to cover all hazards, while the term *caution* is never used. Be sure to keep the users' expectations in mind when you are deciding how to present information on hazards. Whatever choice is made, it should be applied consistently across *all* procedures.

18.5   Place warnings and cautions on the same page as and immediately before the step to which they apply.

Summary

Place warnings and cautions immediately before the step to which they refer to increase the probability that the user will read the warning or caution. Also, to help the user find and recall a warning or caution more easily, place warnings and cautions on the same page as the related step. Repeat warnings or cautions for all applicable steps of the procedure.

Discussion

Warnings and cautions must be placed immediately prior to the step to which they refer (Fuchs, Engelschall, & Imlay, 1981; Wogalter, Godfrey, & Fontenelle, 1987). Placing the warning or caution before the associated step will reduce the likelihood that an error will occur because a user is performing a step while unaware of a related hazard. Procedure users must be aware of cautionary information and potential hazards before they perform an action that may put someone or something in danger. Warnings and cautions should also be on the same page as the step so that the user has all the information needed to execute that step safely. If the warning or caution is on one page and the action is on the next page, the user may recall the cautionary information incorrectly or even forget it.

Warnings and cautions should also be presented every time they apply to a step. For example, if a particular caution regarding engine temperature is applicable to both Step **[8]** and Step **[25]**, then the caution should be placed before each step. Warnings and cautions should be repeated as many times as needed throughout a procedure, but they should not be overused, or procedure users may begin to ignore them.

18.6   Use notes to present supplemental information.

Summary

Much of the information that has been stated previously about warnings and cautions is applicable to notes as well. Notes provide supplemental information in procedures that is different from the information in warnings and cautions. Therefore, notes should look different from warnings and cautions.

Discussion

Notes are used to provide supplemental information in procedures and are qualitatively different from warnings and cautions. Notes provide additional information that, while useful, is not essential to performing a procedural task safely. Whereas warnings and cautions provide critical information that must be adhered to in order to prevent injury or equipment damage, the information in notes is not as critical.

Notes can be used in several situations:

- Notes can emphasize important information, such as parameters related to Technical Specifications.

- Notes can inform users of an expected situation in the facility. For example, a note could inform users that power to a piece of equipment will be interrupted when a circuit breaker is removed. If the expected situation may be dangerous, use a warning or caution to convey the information instead.

- Notes can provide location information regarding equipment.

- Notes can group steps if section headings are not adequate for this purpose. For example, if a group of steps presents prestart criteria for a pump, you could indicate this fact in a note preceding the first step in the group.

The example below illustrates how a note can be formatted in a procedure. Notice how the note is emphasized by lines above and below. This technique differentiates notes from cautions, which (in the examples presented here) are boxed in their entirety.

Note

Overriding an AFAS when the steam generator level is less
than 0% wr may cause a loss of heat removal.

Much of the information presented in the previous sections regarding warnings and
cautions applies to notes as well. Notes must be clear, concise, and unambiguous.
A unique format should be used to draw attention to notes. However, a note is not
as critical to user performance as a warning or caution. Therefore, the unique
format of notes should distinguish the notes from warnings and cautions and need
not contain as much emphasis as the format for warnings or cautions.

As with warnings and cautions, a note should be placed just prior to and on the
same page as the step to which it applies. Placing notes before an associated
action allows the users to see the supplemental information before they perform
the associated action.

Finally, actions should not be included in notes. Actions belong in steps. Just as
with warnings and cautions, do not hide actions in notes by using the passive
voice. Users can easily overlook actions if they are not presented as steps.

Chapter 19

Cross-References

Most procedures should be written in a step-by-step format. The user reads a step, performs it, and then repeats the process for the next step. However, not all steps in procedures can be placed within this sequential (linear) flow of steps; sometimes it is necessary or advantageous to use cross-references to direct the user to depart from the normal linear flow of information. Cross-references instruct users to go to a specific step in a procedure; an example of a cross-reference is *IF header temperature is above 230°C, THEN GO TO Step [4] in this procedure.*

Several types of cross-references can be distinguished. It is useful to draw distinctions between (1) explicit and implicit cross-references, (2) references and branches, (3) conditional and unconditional cross-references, and (4) internal and external cross-references.

- *Explicit* cross-references specifically direct the user to refer to another procedure or another part of the same procedure. *Implicit* cross-references are not stated in the procedure; users are expected to know that a cross-reference is necessary.

- *References* direct the user to temporarily abandon his or her place in the current (i.e, base) procedure, perform the cross-referenced steps, and then return to the base procedure, typically beginning with the step following the cross-reference instruction. *Branches* direct the procedure user to abandon permanently the current procedure (or place in the current procedure) and to go to another place in the procedure set for instructions.

- An *unconditional* cross-reference is always performed. A *conditional* cross-reference is only performed when certain specified conditions are met. Conditional cross-references are specified in conditional statements.

- *Internal* cross-references send the user to a step that lies within the procedure containing the cross-referencing statement. *External* cross-references send the user to a step that lies within another procedure.

Figure 19.1 provides examples of these different types of cross-references. No examples of implicit cross-references are provided because they are not included in the text and thus, by definition, have no format.

As will be discussed in Section 19.2, use of cross-references should be minimized; if possible, cross-references should be eliminated altogether. Cross-references are a necessary evil in complex procedures, such as those used in nuclear power plants, that may not be necessary in simpler procedures. If your procedures are sufficiently simple that you can avoid using cross-references or can restrict use of cross-references to one type (e.g., internal conditional references to additional information), then do so.

This chapter discusses four principles applicable to cross-references:

- Use explicit cross-references whenever possible.

- Minimize cross-references.

- Write cross-references that provide all necessary information in a usable, consistent format.

- Pay special attention to cross-references and cross-referenced material whenever documents are revised or updated.

19.1   Use explicit cross-references whenever possible.

Summary

Do not expect users to know that a cross-reference is necessary. Whenever possible, include cross-references explicitly in procedures.

Discussion

Cross-references are actions and, like all actions, they should be specified clearly and unambiguously. Few procedure writers would write a step like *Open the valve* without specifying which valve; yet, procedure users are sometimes instructed to perform a task without being told that additional guidance on performing that task exists in another procedure. In both of these cases, the procedure places unreasonable demands on its users by not alerting them to useful information.

Type of Cross-Reference	Basic Format of Step
Internal Unconditional Reference	REFER TO Step [step number] in this procedure. RETURN TO [step number] in this procedure.
External Unconditional Reference	REFER TO Step [step number] in [procedure name and number]. RETURN TO [step number] in this procedure.
Internal Conditional Reference	<u>IF</u> condition X exists, <u>THEN</u> REFER TO Step [step number] in this procedure. RETURN TO [step number] in this procedure.
External Conditional Reference	<u>IF</u> condition X exists, <u>THEN</u> REFER TO Step [step number] in [procedure name and number]. RETURN TO [step number] in this procedure.
Internal Unconditional Branch	GO TO Step [step number] in this procedure.
External Unconditional Branch	GO TO Step [step number] in [procedure name, and number].
Internal Conditional Branch	<u>IF</u> condition X exists, <u>THEN</u> GO TO Step [step number] in this procedure.
External Conditional Branch	<u>IF</u> condition X exists <u>THEN</u> GO TO Step [step number] in [procedure name and number].

Figure 19.1. Examples of Explicit Cross-References. Examples of the different types of explicit cross-references are shown.

Implicit cross-references can become especially problematic when users are required to perform a task that is described in *several* different procedures without the aid of explicit cross-references to those procedures. They may be expected to know that they perform Section 4.5 of this procedure, Section 4.11 of another procedure, all of a third procedure, and scattered steps from a fourth procedure. To avoid this problem, cross-references should be explicit whenever possible—the procedure should specifically say, *REFER TO Section 4.0 of this procedure* or *IF the valve body is corroded, <u>THEN</u> REFER TO Appendix A of this procedure.*

Implicit cross-references are often fostered when procedures are based on systems rather than tasks. For example, at a power generating facility, there may be a procedure for the main turbine, the various sections of which discuss starting the turbine, operating the turbine, shutting the turbine down, and maintaining the turbine when it is shut down. This procedure would seldom (if ever) be performed from start to finish, because there would be no reason to start the turbine, run it for a while, and then shut it down. Instead, various sections of the procedure are performed as necessary. For example, when the reactor is started up, the start-up section of the main turbine procedure is performed—along with sections of many other procedures that govern the start-up of the reactor itself and the many auxiliary systems that support reactor operations. Because these procedures are written without consideration of the tasks that will be performed, they do not include the explicit cross-references that would be necessary to direct the performance of those tasks; all cross-references are implicit. This situation reduces the usefulness of procedures, because of the usability problems involved with using many procedures at once and the likelihood that users will overlook a procedure that applies and perform some actions from memory, perhaps incorrectly.

One obvious way to address such a problem is to include explicit cross-references that direct the performance of the many different procedures necessary to perform the complex task. These cross-references could be included in the various procedures or in a separate procedure that directs the performance of the complex task. While this may be an improvement, it does not address the fundamental problem—instructions for performing the task are scattered through several procedures. Instead of making the implicit cross-references explicit, the best solution is to develop procedures that address tasks that are actually performed. Thus, in this example, the solution would be to develop a task-oriented procedure (or a set of task-oriented procedures) that addresses reactor start-up (and only reactor start-up) and consolidates all the information that was formerly scattered among procedures.

This solution can create document control problems, however. If procedures address tasks rather than systems, it is likely that some information will be repeated in several procedures. For instance, information regarding turbine operation may now have to be incorporated in several different task-oriented procedures, where it was formerly only in the system-oriented turbine procedure. While this duplication will make the user's job easier, it can complicate the procedure writer's, as any revision must now be made in several procedures rather than simply one.

Fortunately, automation can simplify this (and many other) aspects of procedure management. Some technical publishing systems, which are sophisticated word processing systems for complex technical documents, allow the development of document databases. A document database can allow a procedure to be assembled from a database of steps. These steps appear only once in the database. If one step is changed, every procedure in which that step appears is automatically changed. A complete discussion of this evolving technology is beyond the scope of this book; see James (1985) for more information. You may also wish to contact various software vendors to learn more about the actual capabilities of various technical publishing systems.

19.2   Minimize cross-references.

Summary

Minimize cross-references; however, cross-references may be necessary to ensure technical accuracy and to simplify complex conditional information. As a general rule, unconditional cross-references should be avoided unless an unconditional external cross-reference allows the procedure user flexibility in coordinating the execution of several procedures. Conditional cross-references, used effectively, can simplify movement through a procedure or set of procedures.

Discussion

This section begins by discussing the problems that are likely to arise when cross-references are used, then discusses one aim of cross-references—to simplify the logic in the procedure. The following sections discuss the use of conditional and unconditional cross-references.

Problems with Cross-References

Cross-references are common in commercial nuclear power plant procedures (Barnes & Radford, 1987; NRC, 1982) and other industries where procedures are used to operate and maintain especially complex equipment. Problems with cross-references are also common. For example, a General Accounting Office Report states that to diagnose and repair one aircraft radar malfunction a technician had to refer to 41 different places in eight documents (Duffy, 1985). Even if in such a case the documents were organized to provide an easy-to-follow path through the 41 different places where the necessary information resided, such excessive cross-referencing would be more difficult than using a single procedure.

Procedure users can have difficulties coordinating procedure steps when cross-references require them to execute multiple series of steps concurrently. However, even cross-references that do not require the concurrent execution of steps can lead to problems associated with the sequencing of actions. Specifically, when users are forced to bounce around through a procedure or, especially, through a set of procedures, technical errors can occur, particularly if steps are skipped. Cross-references can also disrupt the flow of information from the procedure to the user. In addition to these problems, cross-references can create placekeeping problems for users and they can create substantial problems for writers in document revision and control (see Section 19.4).

Barnes and Radford (1987, pp. 29-30) describe how nuclear power plant operators feel about cross-references in operating procedures:

> Operators reported that plant procedures are designed so that operators are frequently required to follow two or more procedures simultaneously. In attempting to use multiple procedures, the operators reported (1) problems in determining how to coordinate steps in the different procedures, (2) difficulties in placekeeping in the procedures, and (3) problems with physically handling more than one procedure manual at a time. The operators stated that these problems had, at times, left them lost among procedures and confused, and that the press of events sometimes required them to abandon efforts to use the procedures and to conduct their tasks on the basis of training and experience alone.

Using Cross-References to Guide Movement Through the Procedure

The best solution to many of these potential problems is to minimize the use of cross-references. Unconditional cross-referencing should almost always be avoided, though eliminating all unconditional cross-references may be impossible or inadvisable. In general, it is better to repeat steps and make procedures longer than to force users to hunt out cross-referenced material; but obviously there are limits. The price of purging unnecessary cross-references is longer procedures, because instructions must be repeated rather than cross-referenced. Thus, the length of potentially cross-referenced passages is one factor that should be evaluated when considering the use of cross-references. Short passages should generally be included in the base procedure, while it may be advantageous to cross-reference longer passages.

While minimizing cross-references is an obvious way to avoid the problems they cause, occasions do exist when cross-references are the lesser evil. Pragmatic issues must certainly be considered when evaluating the degree of cross-referencing appropriate in a procedure set. For example, one must question whether the procedure will be performed by an individual or by a team. A team should be able to handle several procedures concurrently more successfully than an individual. Cross-references should be used only when absolutely necessary if the procedures are to be executed under stressful situations and time constraints, conditions that can be expected to increase the errors made when cross-references are performed. The amount of lay-down space for procedures must be considered, lest the user end up with one procedure on the table, one in his or her lap, and one tucked under an arm. Also, if a task is performed locally, it is obviously not advantageous to require users to lug an armful of procedures to the worksite.

Also, the problems associated with cross-references can increase as cross-referenced steps are nested within other cross-referenced steps. Thus, it appears advisable to repeat even lengthy portions of procedures rather than cross-reference them, if doing so eliminates multiple levels of cross-referencing.

If it is necessary to include cross-references in a procedure, provide the simplest path possible through the logic under the most likely set of conditions. Construct steps so that (1) it will be easy to follow the logic of the steps, (2) the steps will make sense to the user, and (3) wasted motions will be minimized.

Decisions about when to use cross-references cannot be made in a vacuum at the writer's desk. The writer will need to consider information about the task, feedback from users, and the results of validation exercises to determine when the benefits of cross-references outweigh their costs. This fact is especially true in the case of conditional cross-references. Decisions about when to use and how to construct conditional cross-references can be very complex. In particular, in some procedures it is impossible to avoid internal conditional branches. However, in such cases, the writer still retains considerable control over how the cross-references will be structured. Although the writer may not minimize the cross-references in the *written* procedure, he or she can minimize how often the cross-references will need to be performed when a procedure is executed and control the complexity of the path through the procedure. Thus, the writer focuses on minimizing cross-references and the complex cross-referencing structures in the *procedure's execution* rather than in the written document itself.

Unconditional Cross-References

As a general rule, unconditional references and branches should be avoided. If the procedure user must always make a transition, then it is generally best to simply include the target steps in the procedure—why make the user make the transition *every* time? However, external unconditional references are sometimes necessary. Some tasks for which procedures are necessary require that many tasks be conducted in tandem. In some cases, the procedure writer will be in a position to determine a good way of integrating the tasks and all of the tasks can be presented in a single series of steps. In other cases, however, the procedure users may be in a better position than the procedure writers to determine how to best integrate the tasks. In this case, external unconditional cross-references lead the user to necessary instructions while giving the user some latitude in how the different sets of instructions will be coordinated.

Conditional Cross-References

Conditional references and branches, either internal or external, can often be useful. Long series of actions may be contingent on complex combinations of conditions. Every path created through the possible combinations of conditions may have unique associated actions. In such cases, explicit cross-references may well be essential to direct the user through the complex path of logic. For example, in Figure 19.2 cross-referencing has been inappropriately avoided at the expense of creating an extremely long and complex step.

---

[1]   IF the torus temperature is less than 110°F,
AND any ERV is open
AND any MSIV is open,
OR
IF the torus temperature is less than 110°F
AND the drywell pressure is less than 3.5 psig
AND any MSIV is open,
THEN bypass the low-low water level MSIV isolation interlocks.

[2]   Stop all operating RCPs.

Figure 19.2. Complex Step. This difficult-to-understand step can be simplified by the use of cross-referencing, as shown in Figure 19.3.

This step can be simplified by breaking it into two steps and using internal conditional branches to direct the user's movement through those steps and subsequent related steps. One example of how this could be done is shown in Figure 19.3.

---

[1]   IF the torus temperature is greater than or equal to 110°F
THEN GO TO Step [4] in this procedure.

[2]   IF all MSIVs are closed,
THEN GO TO Step [4] in this procedure.

[3]   IF any ERV is open
OR the drywell pressure is less than 3.5 psig
THEN bypass the low-low water level MSIV isolation interlocks.

[4]   Stop all operating RCPs.

Figure 19.3. Use of Cross-Referencing to Simplify a Step. Here, Figure 19.2 is simplified by breaking one step into three and using cross-referencing. The logic here is equivalent and easier to follow. Note how conditions have been stated positively rather than using NOT; for instance, this improved example uses *greater than or equal to 110°F* instead of *NOT less than 110°F* and *MSIVs are closed* instead of *MSIVs are NOT open.*

Restructuring the long complex step into multiple steps, with explicit conditional branches to direct movement through the steps, simplifies the original long complex step in a number of ways. First, all problems of potential ambiguity associated with the use of <u>AND</u> and <u>OR</u> within a single conditional statement can be eliminated (see Section 17.3). Also, note how the improved construction in Figure 19.3 moves the common necessary conditions (torus temperature less than 110°F and any MSIV being open) to the beginning of the step series. If these conditions are not met, the user is directed to skip past the rest of the (now) irrelevant conditional information. This second feature of conditional branches is perhaps their greatest value; they allow for the user to skip past additional conditional information that has been determined to be irrelevant, saving time and simplifying procedure execution (Brooke & Duncan, 1981).

Conditional internal branches should be used when they simplify the presentation of complex conditional information, as in the example above. However, considerable care should be taken to ensure that the cross-references provide the simplest and clearest path possible through the complex information. For example, common necessary conditions can be presented early in the series, as in the previous example. Also, cross-references to short procedure segments are generally preferred to repeating the steps when users must conditionally perform a sequence of steps and when conditions under which they will perform the cross-referenced steps are unlikely. On the other hand, if users will likely need to perform a series of conditional steps, it is probably better to include them in the procedure and require users to skip around the steps when the conditions do not apply. That is to say, when deciding whether to repeat steps or cross-reference the steps, design the procedure so that it is easiest to use most of the time.

An additional caveat should be mentioned here, however. The complexity of the logic should not be evaluated in a vacuum, but in light of what is known about the operational setting in which the procedure will be used. For example, the simplest possible logic sequence may not be better than a slightly more complex sequence if the complex sequence provides a better match with the user's understanding of the situation. Also, the configuration of the operational setting should be considered. You might, for example, want to have an operator check gauges on one side of the control room first and then move to the other side to check additional gauges, rather than having him or her go back and forth across the control room, even if doing so makes for a slightly more complex series of conditional steps.

Often procedures that contain many cross-references can be presented more clearly in flowcharts. Thus, when faced with a procedure that seems to demand the use of many cross-references, consider using a flowchart if that option is available. Section 20.4 introduces the advantages of flowcharts.

One final point should be made about the need to minimize cross-references. Sometimes cross-references are included in procedures not to aid procedure users, but for the benefit of procedure writers. It may seem easier to write and maintain a large set of interrelated procedures when instructions for specific tasks are presented in the series in a single place, and referenced as necessary, rather than repeated in many procedures. However, as discussed in Section 19.4, cross-referencing can create its own problems in document control and revision. Carefully consider whether cross-references solve more problems than they create when considering their use to simplify document production and maintenance.

19.3   Write cross-references that provide all necessary information in a usable, consistent format.

Summary

Key words should be used to define each type of cross-reference. These key words should be emphasized (i.e., coded). The structure of conditional cross-references should be coded through use of white space. Cross-referenced steps should be fully identified. All cross-references should identify the specific steps to which the user should go (or refer).

Discussion

The format of cross-references can have a pronounced effect on their usability. Cross-references should provide complete and clear information on where the cross-referenced information is located and, for conditional cross-references, on the conditions under which the cross-reference should be performed. As much detail as possible should be provided about the location of the cross-referenced steps. For example, the instructions to perform a cross-reference should identify the referenced step with information such as the name and number of the procedure containing the step, the number of the step itself, and, if possible, the page number where the step is located. Presumably, revision numbers and dates are not necessary to ensure that the user accesses the most recent revision of the cross-referenced procedure (other document control measures should ensure that users receive current revisions of procedures). However, the inclusion of revision numbers and dates does serve an essential purpose in document control, as discussed in Section 19.4.

In addition to this location information, the step must provide any conditional information that dictates whether the referenced material should be cross-referenced and also provide instructions about how the cross-reference is to be performed. For example, if users are to navigate through the procedure correctly, they must know whether they are performing a reference (which will require that they mark or note the location to which they must return) or a branch. Information that dictates the conditions under which a cross-reference is to be performed must be presented up front—before the cross-referencing instructions—and it must be as clear and explicit as possible. If it is presented after the reference (e.g., *Go to Step [3] but only if . . .*), the user may erroneously perform a conditional cross-reference before reading that it should only be performed under certain conditions.

The clarity of both the conditional information and the cross-referencing instructions can be enhanced by designing and adhering to specific formats. Rules should be followed for presenting conditional information to ensure consistent and clear presentation. For example, conditional terms should be used and the rules of formal logic should be followed when presenting conditional references and branches (see Chapter 17). Formatting can also code each type of cross-reference to signal information to the procedure user about the cross-reference. Coding can be achieved with verbal, typographical, and spatial cues; see Section 13.1.

Verbal cues consist of key words that alert the reader as to the type of cross-reference encountered. For example, references could always be indicated with the words *REFER TO . . . while continuing in this procedure*. Branches could be indicated with the phrase GO TO. If branches are used to indicate that the base procedure should be permanently or temporarily abandoned, key words should provide this information as well (e.g., *Abandon this procedure permanently and GO TO . . .* or *Abandon this procedure temporarily and GO TO . . .*).

Typographical cues consist of conventions such as the use of italics, bold type, and different fonts. Spatial cues use both the relative position of elements and the white space created by the positioning to create signals. Spatial cues can be created by using line breaks and indentation to set apart specific pieces of information. These verbal, typographical, and spatial cues are most effective when users are trained to understand their meaning, when cues are used sparingly, and when cues are not overly complex (Duchastel, 1982).

In the following example, a variety of cues are provided for the procedure user. The step format shown uses only techniques that can be accomplished with a standard typewriter or word processor; elaborate desktop publishing technology is not required to present cross-referencing steps clearly.

> **[17]**   IF the computer fails to retrieve the data,
> THEN REFER TO procedure 201b, "Manual Data Recovery,"
> Steps 5 through 9 inclusively, beginning on page 3, while
> continuing in this procedure. Observe the note that precedes
> Step 5.

In the example, typographical cues (capitalization and underlining) signal the organization of the IF. . . THEN conditional statement that provides the conditional information in this step. The organization of this conditional statement is clarified by the way in which it is positioned on the page. The THEN clause begins on a new line directly below the IF clause. The cross-reference is signaled typographically with capitalization and verbally with the phrase REFER TO.

19.4   Pay special attention to cross-references and cross-referenced material whenever documents are revised or updated.

Summary

A system should be in place to track how all documents in a set are linked through cross-references. Whenever a document is revised, the accuracy of identification information in cross-references to that document (e.g., step numbers) must be verified. If necessary, the procedure should be reverified and revalidated.

Discussion

Cross-references can easily introduce errors in procedures when those procedures are revised. This problem is somewhat ironic, as cross-references are often used in an attempt to prevent errors from being made when procedures are revised. The use of cross-references can reduce the risk of errors in procedure revisions because the cross-references eliminate redundant passages in procedures, and thus help ensure that passages in need of revision are not overlooked. However, revisions in a procedure that affect aspects of the procedure, such as its name, number, or its step numbering sequence, are problematic if that procedure can be entered from other procedures via cross-references. These types of changes affect the features of a cross-referenced step that identify it in cross-references in other procedures. Thus, whenever a procedure is revised in a manner that changes such features, it is necessary to verify every cross-referencing step to that procedure throughout the procedure set.

Further, in a procedure where all steps are performed sequentially and no cross-references are used, it is only necessary to verify one path through the procedure. In a highly branched procedure there are many paths through the procedure and it becomes necessary to confirm that all paths are complete and that no path violates any pre-conditional information as it snakes through the procedure set. Each additional conditional cross-reference in a procedure creates a new path that a user can follow through the procedure. In addition to potentially bypassing important information, the complex structures created by conditional cross-references can lead to errors by introducing steps that change the dynamics of the system in ways that were not anticipated when other "down stream" steps were written (without the knowledge of what steps would be introduced up stream through some unusual combination of conditional cross-references). Thus, to be absolutely sure that no revision creates a problem in a procedure, writers must not only revalidate and reverify a procedure subsequent to a major revision, but revalidate and reverify every procedure that cross-references the modified procedure as well.

Complex structures created by nested cross-references create problems for procedure writers as well as users. It can be very difficult to ensure that a procedure is technically correct under all conditions when it contains complex layers of cross-references. Procedure writers often overlook problems along one or more paths through a procedure even when the structure contains only small amounts of branching (Weiss, 1990). The more complex the web of cross-referencing that ties a set of procedures together, the more likely it is that something will be missed when procedures are revised and verified.

Because of these potential problems, it is essential that a system be used to track how all documents in a set are linked through cross-references. Whenever a document is revised, the accuracy of identification information in cross-references to that document (e.g., step numbers) must be verified. Whenever a document undergoes major revisions, it and all documents linked to it through cross-references should be revalidated.

Chapter 20

Special Types of Steps

Steps should be tailored to the information that they present. A simple step consists of a verb and a direct object (e.g., *Open the relief valve*). In other types of steps, it is necessary to present additional information. For example, conditional steps (e.g., <u>*IF*</u> *header pressure is above 100 psia,* <u>*THEN*</u> *open the relief valve*) must present a condition as well as a verb and an object, and must use conditional terms according to the rules of formal logic.

Other, more complex types of steps, such as the following, have different requirements:

- *Nonsequential steps* are performed out of sequence with other steps. In these steps, in addition to specifying the action that must be performed, it is necessary to specify the criteria that define when the step must be performed. These criteria are typically related to time (e.g., a valve should be closed 10 minutes after it is opened) or to facility parameters (e.g., a valve should be closed once a tank is full). In addition to a step specifying these criteria, the procedure should include some means of reminding operators to perform the step.

- *Verification steps* require users to determine whether a certain criterion is met and, if it is not, to take action to ensure that the criterion is met. Because steps of this sort are common in procedures, a concise, consistent format should be adopted for presenting them.

- *Equally acceptable steps* allow users to choose among alternative actions.

- *Diagnostic steps* present decision criteria that help users diagnose a fault or condition.

- *Immediate operator actions* must be performed without delay in an emergency.

Typically, steps such as these are necessary only in complex procedures, such as those used in nuclear power plants. If you write simpler procedures, the information in this chapter is probably overkill.

The requirements for these steps will be discussed in more detail in the remainder of this chapter. One principle is presented regarding each type of step.

20.1   Use an appropriate format for nonsequential steps (i.e., continuous steps, time-dependent steps, and concurrent steps).

Summary

Nonsequential steps should be presented so they clearly specify the criteria that govern when they should be performed. The nonsequential step should first appear in the procedure at the earliest point where it may apply and should be followed by reminders (e.g., on the facing page) for as long as necessary.

Discussion

A central characteristic of procedures is that they present steps in the order in which those steps must be performed; in fact, *Webster's New Collegiate Dictionary* (1977, p. 917) defines a procedure as "a series of steps followed in a regular definite order." This aspect of procedures greatly simplifies their execution. The procedure user performs Step 1, Step 2, Step 3, and so on, through the last step in the procedure, at which time he or she has completed the task described in the procedure.

It is not always possible to present steps in the order in which they will be performed, however. Four basic reasons can either act alone or conspire to obscure the correct order for the steps in a procedure to be performed: (1) there is technical rationale for allowing users to determine the correct order of step performance, (2) the step should be performed at a time dependent on external system parameters, (3) the step should be performed after a certain period of time has passed, or (4) two or more steps should be performed concurrently.

When presenting a nonsequential step in a procedure, it is important to provide users with the criteria that govern when (or if) the step should be performed. This should be done in the manner that is most appropriate for the type of step, although it is important that similar types of nonsequential steps be presented in a similar manner. It is also important to provide users with reminders to perform the steps; this section also discusses reminders.

Basic Nonsequential Steps

Occasionally, there simply is no rigid order in which the steps must be performed. In these instances, it is simply necessary to indicate to the user that the steps may be performed in any sequence, perhaps by using a note.

The use of these types of nonsequential steps should be limited, however, as they may introduce confusion—users may overlook or omit steps if they are skipping back and forth through the procedure. Unless there is a strong technical reason for allowing steps to be performed in alternative orders, it is generally best to decide on an order and present the steps in that order. If possible, the nonsequential steps should include any criteria that will be useful to users when deciding upon an order for performing the steps.

Continuous Steps

It is possible that the time at which a step must be performed may be dependent not on the completion of the prior step, but on some system parameter; for example, a valve must be closed when a tank is full. These steps are known as *continuous steps*, because users must continuously keep them in mind until they are performed.

When dealing with continuous steps, the procedure writer cannot predict exactly how the system will respond as the procedure is executed, and thus does not know where in the sequence of steps to insert the continuous step. In the example cited, the flow into the tank may be affected by factors that have nothing to do with the particular procedure being executed. Thus, the procedure writer cannot include the step specifying that the valve be closed at the point in the procedure where the valve must be closed.

A continuous step should be presented in the procedure at the point where users may first be required to perform the action. Continuous steps are best presented in conditional statements, as shown in Figure 20.1. The condition in the conditional statement indicates when the action should be performed. The continuous step should be followed by reminders, which are discussed at the end of this section.

Continuous steps can also be recurrent; for example, users may be required to repeatedly fill and drain a tank. In these instances, the step should clearly indicate that the step is to be performed repeatedly.

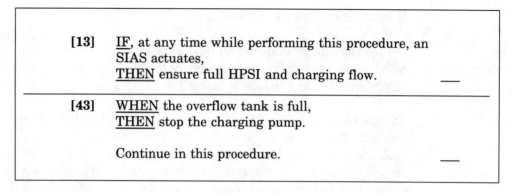

Figure 20.1. Use of Conditional Terms to Present Continuous Steps. These nonsequential steps, which are dependent on system parameters, are best presented using conditional statements. Note the use of the phrase *Continue in this procedure* to indicate that Step **[43]** is not a hold point.

Time-Dependent Steps

Other steps are performed after a set period of time has passed. These steps are called *time-dependent steps*. For instance, a maintainer may be required to notify the shift supervisor 30 minutes after taking a pump off line. Unless the procedure writer knows exactly how many subsequent steps in the procedure the maintainer will perform in 30 minutes, he cannot accurately insert a step into the procedure directing the maintainer to notify his supervisor *at the time the step is read*.

So, when writing a time-dependent step, you must assist the procedure user in tracking the time. It is important to provide space for users to note the time that "starts the clock" and to present a calculation aid that will enable them to calculate the time at which the action should be taken. Figure 20.2 demonstrates one method of presenting this information.

Common sense should be used when deciding whether to incorporate a calculation aid in a time-dependent step. Obviously, if an action must be completed within a brief period of time (e.g., 10 seconds), the calculation is trivial and a calculation aid is unnecessary, although it *is* necessary to clearly state that the action must be performed within 10 seconds.

Time-dependent steps can also be recurrent; for example, users may be required to perform an action *every* 15 minutes. A calculation aid or checklist may also be appropriate in such a situation. Users could check off the action each time it is performed.

When there are many calculated times in a procedure, consider the use of an appendix to log all of the times. If such an appendix is used, procedure users can look up all the relevant times in one place rather than having to flip through the procedures.

NOTE *The following step initiates a time-limited sequence. Steps [2] through [6] are to be performed within 20 minutes.*

[1]   Determine the time by which Step [6] is
          to be completed.   ___

     [1.1]   Record the time that Step [2] is
          to be started.   ___

     [1.2]   Add 20 minutes.   + <u>20 minutes</u>

     [1.3]   Record the time that Step [6] is
          to be completed.   ___

[2]   Place <u>Incident Action</u> switch to TEST.   ___

[3]   Verify amber ALARM TEST light on the
          AIA graphic panel is lit.   ___ ___
                                                                   IV

[4]   REFER TO Steps [20] - [37] in this procedure.
          RETURN TO Step [5].

[5]   Place <u>Incident Action</u> switch to OFF.   ___

[6]   Push RESET pushbutton on AIA logic tester and
          record the correct time.   ___

Figure 20.2. Time-Dependent Steps. This figure demonstrates how a calculation aid can be used to assist users in performing a time-dependent step. This step would be followed on subsequent pages by reminders that the step still applied.

Concurrent Steps

Finally, a procedure may require users to perform tasks concurrently. Figure 20.3 depicts the presentation of concurrent steps.

---

[1]   CONCURRENTLY PERFORM Steps **[2]** and **[3]**.

[2]   Prepare Solution X by performing the following:

    [2.1]   Add 10 grams Compound A to 1000 ml water.   ___

    [2.2]   Heat the water to 200°F.   ___

    [2.3]   Naturally cool the solution to room
             temperature.   ___

[3]   Prepare Solution Z by performing the following:

    [3.1]   Strain Solution Y to remove the sediment.   ___

    [3.2]   Let the sediment air dry to remove any
             moisture.   ___

    [3.3]   Crush the sediment with a mortar and pestle.   ___

    [3.4]   Mix 50 grams of the sediment with 1000 ml
             water.   ___

[4]   Combine Solution X with Solution Z.   ___

Figure 20.3. Concurrent Steps. In this example, users are instructed to perform Steps **[2]** and **[3]** concurrently. Compare with Figure 20.4.

The concurrent performance of tasks may lead to problems, as users who are required to do too much simultaneously may forget to perform actions. One method of avoiding concurrent steps is to break the concurrent steps into actions that can be presented sequentially, as shown in Figure 20.4.

There are advantages and disadvantages to the approaches used in Figure 20.3 and 20.4. The best way to present this type of information depends on the nature of the tasks being described. As a general rule, concurrent steps should be avoided, because of the potential for error. This potential can be exacerbated if users are performing more than one procedure at once. Yet, it may be difficult to integrate the individual steps that comprise each task into a single sequence of steps, either for technical reasons or simply because the resulting sequence of steps is unclear.

> [1]   Add 10 grams of Compound A to 1000 ml water
>   to make Solution X.   —
>
> [2]   Heat Solution X to 200°F.   —
>
> [3]   While Solution X is heating, strain Solution Y to
>   remove the sediment.   —
>
> [3]   Naturally cool Solution X to room temperature.   —
>
> [4]   While Solution X is cooling, let the sediment from
>   Solution Y air dry to remove any moisture.   —
>
> [5]   Crush the sediment from Solution Y with a mortar
>   and pestle.   —
>
> [6]   Mix 50 grams of the sediment from Solution Y
>   with 1000 ml water to make Solution Z.   —
>
> [7]   Combine Solution X with Solution Z.   —

Figure 20.4. Concurrent Steps Broken Up. Here, Steps **[2]** and **[3]** from Figure 20.3 are broken up and combined into a single sequence of steps. Although this procedure no longer includes concurrent steps, it may be more difficult to understand because the steps are wordier and do not appear in context.

In Figure 20.4, the steps may appear fragmented and out of context. Although, users performing the steps by rote may do better with Figure 20.4, experienced users may desire the contextual grouping provided in Figure 20.3.

The procedure writer must decide on the best way to present concurrent steps. Consider the experience level and desire of users when making such decisions, and verify them during verification and validation. The writers' guide should provide the necessary guidance to support these decisions.

The Importance of Reminders

Thus far, this section has discussed the initial presentation of nonsequential steps (i.e., the step itself). It is important that the step be followed by reminders to operators to perform the nonsequential action. Figure 20.5 presents examples of the types of reminders that may be used.

The placement and emphasis of these reminders is important. They should appear in a consistent location on every page. Potential locations include the top of each page or the facing page. They should also be emphasized so that they stand out, but they should not be unduly emphasized so that they detract from the emphasis of other, more important information on the page, such as cautions. Figure 20.6 demonstrates placement on the facing page.

Continue to cycle pressurizer heaters every 15 minutes.

Notify the shift supervisor that the recirculation pump has been taken off line by the time noted in Step **[16]** in this procedure.

<u>IF</u>, at <u>any</u> time while performing this procedure, an SIAS actuates, <u>THEN</u> ensure full HPSI and charging flow.

Figure 20.5. Examples of Reminders to Perform Nonsequential Steps. Reminders such as these should follow nonsequential steps when necessary. They should appear in a consistent location on each page (e.g., on the top of the page or on the facing page) and should be emphasized in an appropriate manner.

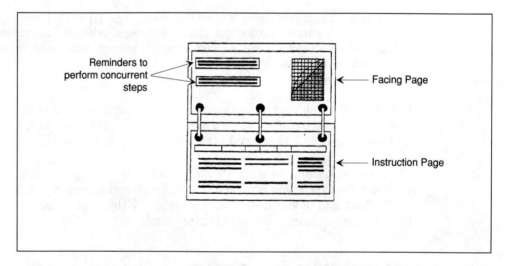

Figure 20.6. Facing Page. The facing page is the page opposite the procedure page. It can be used to present supplementary information, such as reminders to perform concurrent steps.

20.2   Use a unique format for verification steps.

Summary

Verification steps should be presented in a consistent manner that clearly conveys the difference between verification steps (1) where users take action to ensure that the condition to be verified is met and (2) where users stop executing the procedure if the condition is not met.

Discussion

Verification steps require operators to verify that a certain condition is met. Because verification steps can be common in procedures and can be especially problematic, they deserve special attention. There are two types of verification steps:

- In the first type, users (1) check if something is so; (2) if it is so, then go on; and (3) if it is not so, then make it so and go on.

- In the second type, users (1) check if something is so; (2) if it is so, then continue in the procedure; and (3) if it is not so, then stop executing the procedure and inform their supervisor.

Verification steps can be presented in a variety of ways, as shown in Figure 20.7.

[1]	Verify open/open Valve A.	___
[1]	<u>IF</u> Valve A is closed, <u>THEN</u> open Valve A.	___
[1]	Ensure that Valve A is open.	___
[1]	Insure that Valve A is open.	___
[1]	Assure that Valve A is open.	___
[1]	Check that Valve A is open.	___

Figure 20.7. A Variety of Ways of Presenting Verification Steps. Although verification steps can be presented in a variety of ways, it is best to decide on a consistent means of presenting them. The first and second examples, while unambiguous, are wordy. The remaining four examples present the information concisely, but users must understand the meaning of the verb.

Because verification steps occur commonly in most types of procedures, a consistent and concise format should be established for each type of verification step. Users encountering such a varied presentation of similar information in a procedure may attribute differences in meaning to spurious differences in presentation, may be unable to distinguish the one or two true differences in meaning lying behind the many differences in presentation, or both. It is best to choose and stick to one means of presenting each type of verification step.

20.3   Minimize equally acceptable steps; when presenting these steps, do so using a unique format.

Summary

Equally acceptable steps should be minimized, as the presentation of unnecessary alternatives clutters the procedure and makes it more difficult to use. Present alternatives only when necessary. Provide criteria for distinguishing among alternatives when possible.

Discussion

Equally acceptable steps are steps where "any one of several alternative steps or sequences of steps may be equally correct" (NRC, 1982, p. 23). When encountering these steps, users may choose among these alternatives.

Equally acceptable steps should be minimized. There will typically be more than one way of accomplishing a task, as many of the systems documented by procedure writers include redundancies and backups. Hence, in some procedures, it would be possible to present different, equally acceptable methods of accomplishing the same objectives for many of the tasks presented in the procedure. The result, however, would be a cluttered, confusing procedure that would continuously be presenting alternatives and requiring the users to make choices among them when such choices are unnecessary.

Procedure writers should limit the use of equally acceptable steps by presenting alternatives only in certain cases. One instance where it may be useful to present alternatives is when the procedure writer has reason to believe that the preferred alternative may not be available. Or, the presentation of equally acceptable steps may be considered a level-of-detail issue; if the procedure writer has reason to believe that an alternative may be useful to users and that they may not be aware of that alternative, then equally acceptable steps may be appropriate.

When alternatives are presented, it is often useful to present criteria that users may use when deciding among these alternatives. In such an instance, equally acceptable steps are best presented as conditional steps, as shown in Figure 20.8.

[18]   IF Pump A is operating,
THEN use Pump A to fill the holding
tank.   ___

IF NOT, THEN use Pump B to fill the holding
tank.   ___

Figure 20.8. Use of a Conditional Statement to Present Equally Acceptable Alternatives. The use of a conditional statement clearly indicates that Pump A is the preferable alternative.

If neither of the alternatives is better than the other but it is still beneficial to provide users with alternatives, then an approach should be used that clearly indicates that only one alternative should be followed. Figure 20.9 shows such an approach.

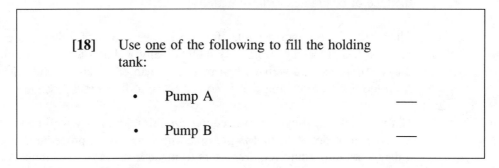

[18]   Use one of the following to fill the holding
tank:

•   Pump A   ___

•   Pump B   ___

Figure 20.9. Equally Acceptable Alternatives. In this case, there is no clear preference between Pump A or Pump B.

20.4   Use an appropriate format for diagnostic steps.

Summary

It is important that procedures assist users in event or fault diagnosis. Because step-by-step procedures are not always the best format for diagnostic procedures, procedure writers should consider using flowcharts to present diagnostic steps.

Discussion

Diagnostic steps are likely to appear in emergency or troubleshooting procedures. As the name implies, diagnostic steps help users determine the status of equipment or a system or the cause of a situation by presenting a series of questions.

Humans are poor diagnosticians. The difficulties humans have when performing diagnoses stem from the difficulty we tend to have with decision making in general. Many researchers have investigated human decision making (e.g., Tversky & Kahneman, 1982). Several factors tend to make decision making difficult for us. We have difficulty accurately assessing probability or risk in uncertain situations; for example, people are unfamiliar with the statistical concept of regression to the mean, which predicts that, among other things, a football team having an exceptionally good season is more likely to have a worse season the following year. We place undue emphasis on information we are familiar with; for example, because airline crashes are covered so extensively by the mass media, we may overestimate our chance of being involved in such a crash. We tend to make decisions early in a process and then seek out information that reinforces those decisions, paying little heed to contradictory information; for instance, at Three Mile Island, operators misdiagnosed the situation and clung to that misdiagnosis in the face of contradictory information.

Thus, one of the important roles for procedures is that of a diagnostic aid that reduces these types of errors. By methodically walking the user through the diagnostic process, a well-written procedure can eliminate much human fallibility from the decision making that is so central to a diagnostic procedure.

Unfortunately, step-by-step procedures are not particularly well-suited to presenting the type of information that is presented in a diagnostic procedure. By its nature, a diagnostic procedure requires users to make a series of decisions. In step-by-step procedures, decision criteria and associated actions are typically presented in conditional statements. Although conditional statements are the best format for presenting this type of information, they can lead to error, particularly when combined with cross-references (e.g., *IF Condition A exists, THEN GO TO Step [5] in this procedure*).

Flowcharts can be less confusing than conditional statements for presenting diagnostic information; instead of dealing with a complex series of conditional statements, users simply trace a path through the flowchart or diagram. Figure 20.10 shows a simple IF . . . THEN statement and an equivalent portion of a flowchart. Granted, Figure 20.10 shows a simple case where there is little possibility for error; but, in a more complex procedure, such as that shown in Figure 20.11, the possibility for error becomes very real indeed. Figure 20.12, an equivalent flowchart, is easier to follow.

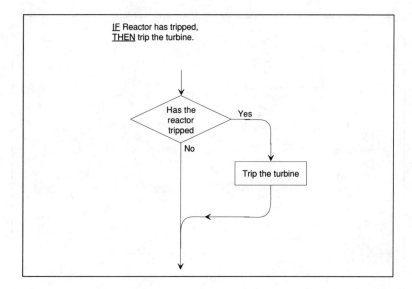

Figure 20.10. An <u>IF</u> . . . <u>THEN</u> Statement and a Corresponding Portion of a Flowchart.
When executing the written step procedure, users must mentally skip over the action if the
condition is not true. When executing the flowchart, users remain on a flowline whether the
condition is true or false; they do not skip anything (adapted from Barnes et al., 1989).

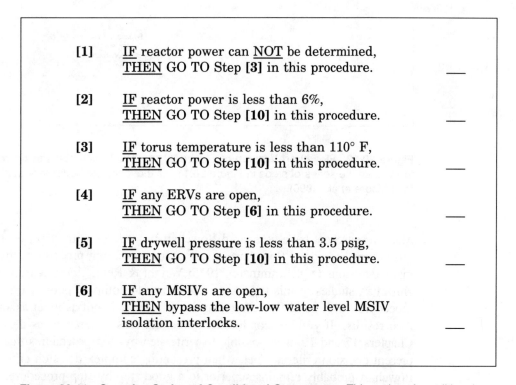

Figure 20.11. Complex Series of Conditional Statements. This series of conditional
statements can be difficult to follow. Compare this figure with the flowchart in Figure 20.12
(adapted from Moore et al., 1990).

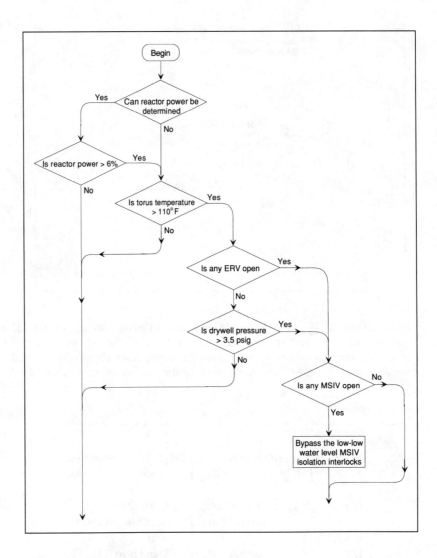

Figure 20.12. Flowchart Version of Figure 20.11. The flowchart in this figure is easier to follow than the series of steps in Figure 20.11, as the logic can be visually traced (adapted from Moore et al., 1990).

Many researchers have compared flowchart procedures with step-by-step procedures and found flowcharts superior for presenting procedures that consist of many decisions (e.g., Kammann, 1975; Wright & Reid, 1973; Wason, 1968). However, studies of this type have a tendency to compare poor step-by-step procedures with good flowcharts, so the difference is not as great as suggested by their results. If you use conditional terms and cross-references as described in Chapters 17 and 19, it is possible to write step-by-step procedures that effectively present decision criteria. Yet, when presenting complex decision criteria, a good flowchart probably remains superior to a good step-by-step procedure. *Techniques for Preparing Flowchart-Format Emergency Operating Procedures* (Barnes et al., 1989) discusses the advantages and disadvantages of flowcharts in greater detail, and also presents guidance for the design of effective flowcharts.

20.5   Include immediate actions in procedures when necessary.

Summary

Immediate actions, which are the initial steps that users take to control an emergency and are performed from memory, should be included in procedures when necessary.

Discussion

Emergency procedures at nuclear power plants and similar facilities typically include immediate operator actions. NUREG-0899, *Guidelines for the Preparation of Emergency Operating Procedures* (NRC, 1982, p. 17), states that immediate operator actions are those actions that operators should take immediately when there are indications of an emergency. These actions are taken to stop further degradation of existing conditions, to mitigate their consequences, and to allow operators to evaluate the situation. Operators normally memorize these actions and perform them without having to refer to an EOP (emergency operating procedure).

The American National Standards Institute provides the following examples of immediate operator actions for reactor operations (American Nuclear Society, 1989, p. 28):

- the verification of automatic actions

- assurance that the reactor is in a safe condition (e.g., shutdown of the reactor with sufficient reactivity margin and establishment of required core cooling)

- notification to plant personnel of the nature of the emergency

- determination that the reactor coolant system pressure boundary is intact

- confirmation of the availability of adequate power sources

- confirmation that containment and exhaust systems are operating properly in order to prevent uncontrolled release of radioactivity.

The list provides an idea of the types of actions that belong in an immediate operator actions section. If you are writing emergency operating procedures in a reactor facility, you can use this list (or other relevant sources) directly. If you are writing procedures (especially emergency procedures) in other types of facilities, determine the actions that must be performed without delay and consider incorporating them in an immediate actions section.

The NRC recommends that immediate operator actions should be included in a procedure as a back-up to user training. This sound guidance should be followed in any procedure that addresses an emergency situation. Immediate operator actions should also be identified as such. Typically, it is sufficient to include them in a section titled, *Immediate Actions*, or in some similar manner.

It should be stressed, however, that inclusion of immediate operator actions in a procedure is not a substitute for training. Because of their critical nature, operators should be able to perform immediate actions without referring to a procedure; the procedure is simply a back-up for operator training in this case.

Part Five: Conclusion

Chapter 21

Some Closing Themes

This book has discussed the principles that govern the preparation of procedures. As a means of wrapping things up, this chapter will discuss some of the themes that have guided the preparation of this book. These themes represent the philosophical approach that lies behind much of the guidance and point out some of the complexities and subtleties of procedure writing.

21.1 The Nature of Writing: Cookbook Versus Craft

This book is not a procedure for writing procedures. Although we have made every effort to make this book useful to the procedure writer and believe that the material presented here will be very helpful to you as you attempt to write better procedures, it is important to understand this limitation—this isn't a cookbook. You can use these principles as a cookbook to a certain extent, but problems will often arise when you try to apply a principle in a unique situation or where two principles conflict with each other. In these situations, you will have to rely on your skills as a writer to sort things out, just as a car mechanic sometimes relies on a sixth sense when fixing an engine or a surgeon sometimes relies on instinct while operating. In this sense, you must sometimes treat procedure writing as a craft rather than a science.

Writers seldom deal with absolutes of right and wrong as do, say, mathematicians. Instead, the writer deals with shades of meaning and subtleties—almost always, there is more than one way to say something. Consider Figure 21.1, which presents several different ways of making the same statement.

Procedure writers do not have the freedom to choose among these many alternatives. Many principles in this book reduce the options you will face when writing a procedure; for example, steps must begin with an action verb, conditional term, or modifier; all action verbs must be taken from an approved list; decision criteria must be written according to the techniques of formal logic; and so on. As a result of these rules, procedures will be more precise, because information is presented in a manner that research or historical practice has shown to be superior and because information is presented consistently.

> We're out of food. I'm going to the store.
>
> We are out of food. I am going to the store.
>
> There's no food in the house, so I'd better go to the store.
>
> I'm going shopping, because there isn't a thing to eat in the house.

Figure 21.1. Different Ways of Saying the Same Thing. There are many different ways to convey the same idea. No one of these ways is correct while the other ways are wrong.

Despite these efforts to increase precision, procedure writers are still working with the English language and cannot be completely freed from its inherent qualities. This fact has important implications for this book and the way you will use it. There are very few absolute rights and wrongs in procedure writing. If there were, we would not have bothered writing this book; instead, we would have simply written a writers' guide for the ultimate procedure and recommended that it be followed. But there is no ultimate procedure. As a procedure writer, you will have to make judgement calls. The purpose of this document is to help you to make those decisions. But do not look to it for proclamations of right or wrong in all situations.

Three examples may clarify this point. One is concerned with type size. Section 11.1 provided a visual angle formula for determining type size. This formula yields a neat, precise numerical answer for the optimal size of type, but this formula alone was not adequate for specifying a type size; line length, font, and other factors that could not be incorporated in the formula had to be considered as well. As a result, typesetters and printers seldom use the visual angle formula; instead, they use their trained eye to determine what looks the best—they approach the issue as a craftsperson, not a scientist.

A second example involves readability formulas. Many researchers have investigated techniques for quantifying how difficult a passage is to read. These formulas are based on sentence length, word length, proportion of words that appear on a list of "simple" words, number of syllables per word, and so on. Like the visual angle formula, readability formulas attempt to quantify an aspect of writing.

And, like the visual angle formula, readability formulas ignore a host of factors that also affect readability but do not lend themselves to quantification. Readability formulas ignore grammar, use of figures and tables, a document's organization and design, and many other factors (Giles, 1990). As discussed throughout this book, these attributes of a document all have an immense effect on its understandability.   Because readability formulas ignore so much, technical communicators discount their usefulness, sometimes in strong language:

> While some authorities recommend readability formulas—if the writer recognizes the formula as a tool limited by the variables manipulated—overwhelming argument from other experts suggests that the formulas should be ignored because they can mislead writers by lulling them into a false sense of security or into writing stilted prose to fit the formula. (Giles, 1990, p. 131)

So, readability formulas are another example of a failure of the cookbook approach. Effective writing cannot be judged by whether the writer got the recipe right, perhaps by using words and sentences of the perfect average length, but must be judged by how well the writer applied his craft.

The third example is concerned with verb choice. It is important that all action verbs in procedures be taken from an approved list (see Section 6.1). When compiling this list, it is important to eliminate redundancy, so that there is a unique, one-to-one correspondence between verbs and actions. This makes perfect sense in the abstract, but in practice it can be difficult to decide when two verbs are redundant and when they are not. For example, do *inform* and *tell* mean the same thing? They do in one sense—both indicate that information is being provided, as in *Inform site management that the reactor has tripped* and *Tell site management that the reactor has tripped*. In this situation, one could be eliminated—probably *inform*, because it is the longer of the two.

However, *tell* can be used in another sense—when instructing someone to do something. Thus, *Tell Chemistry to sample for boron* is another acceptable use of *tell*. But what if a procedure instructs a subordinate to "tell" a superior to do something (e.g., *Tell the shift supervisor to declare a site emergency*)? Depending on the politics at a particular facility, *tell* may not be appropriate in these situations. So should the verb list include another verb, such as *ask*, for situations when subordinates are dealing with superiors? Is the issue worth the complexity of one more verb on the list, and the potential of confusion by users who are not familiar with the difference?

Other connotations of *tell* and *inform* may intrude on matters. *Inform* may be understood by some as implying that the person who informs must ensure that the listener understands (or becomes *informed*). *Tell*, on the other hand, may not carry this implication. Once you have told someone you have done your part; if he doesn't understand, that's his problem. This is a subtle difference, and it may not be apparent or important to everyone. But is it important enough to dictate that both verbs be included in the verb list?

There are no correct or incorrect answers to these questions; the correct answer will depend on the particular situation at a facility. This example demonstrates some of the subtle shades of meaning that affect word use in procedures. These shades of meaning cannot be quantified; instead, they hinge on the feelings that we associate with a word.

The Importance of Training

Our intention in presenting this discussion is not to be discouraging; we are merely being forthright about what this book has to offer. This book will be of much use to you, but you need more—you need some training in technical communication. This training will enable you to develop the skills as a writer—as a craftsperson—that are necessary for applying the guidance presented here in an optimal manner. If you have already had classes such as these, that's good. If you haven't, some training in technical communication could be quite useful to you.

To take the cookbook analogy literally, consider a novice cook and a trained chef who both prepare the same recipe. The trained chef will certainly prepare a tastier, more succulent dish. Why? Because, although both had access to the same recipe, the chef brought years of training and experience to the task and was able to do a better job. Similarly, with some basic skills in technical communication, you can use this book to prepare procedures that are better than those prepared by someone who merely follows this book and does not have the additional training.

Technical communication (or writing) classes are relatively common. They are offered at two- and four-year colleges and may be offered at some vocational schools. If you work at a large facility, perhaps they are offered somewhere on site. You might be able to attend one of these classes or, for a large enough group of procedure writers, it may be possible to arrange a special class.

Don't be too concerned if you are taking a class in technical writing rather than procedure writing. Few classes specifically teach procedure writing. Further, the skills you learn in a technical communication class will be useful to you as a procedure writer—especially when combined with the information in this book. A technical communication class should teach an approach that can be applied to any technical document. This approach should work for procedures as well as any other documents that you prepare.

21.2   Correctness

Procedures must be correct. This point is obvious—an incorrect procedure will lead users to take incorrect actions. As a procedure writer, much of the work you do is intended to keep errors out of procedures—your research into background documents, your subject matter expertise, your interviews with users and subject matter experts, and the validation and verification process are all important in this regard.

A procedure that is correct but is misunderstood is as bad as an incorrect procedure. To take an obvious example, a technically correct procedure that was written in a foreign language would be useless. There are other, more subtle ways that a "correct" procedure may be misunderstood. One occurs when the procedure assumes knowledge that the procedure user does not possess. Say that a procedure writer instructs users to start a pump, but does not include instructions to check for abnormal vibration. Now assume that this procedure is executed by a novice user who fails to check for vibration and the pump is in fact faulty; as a result, an expensive pump is damaged. The user may argue that the procedure was not correct because it omitted instructions to check for vibration, while the procedure writer may argue that the user should have known to do that. Obviously, in situations such as these, arguments over whether the procedure was "correct" are moot; the procedure was not executed successfully, and that is what matters.

Dye (1988) argues that problems such as this render the distinction between correctness and usability meaningless. While this position may be viewed as extreme, correctness and usability must be evaluated as two facets of the same issue. Compromises in usability for the sake of correctness can never be justified.

But it can be dangerous to concentrate too much on correctness: it is possible to try to hold procedures to an arbitrary standard of correctness that is so stringent that we lose sight of the whole point of the procedure. Writing that tries too hard to be correct "haggles over trifles and refuses to know when errors and confusion no longer matter" (Follett, 1966, p. 9). For instance, you don't cross a bridge, you cross a river; you drink a cupful of coffee rather than a cup of coffee. Yet to correct errors at so fine a level is to split hairs with little regard for what really matters—will the reader understand what has been written? There is no ambiguity in either of these expressions, so the answer is yes.

Further, in some cases, an "incorrect" term is preferable to a correct term. For example, a spiral staircase is, technically speaking, a helical staircase, because a spiral exists in only two dimensions while a helix, like a staircase, exists in three dimensions. When a reporter gets a scoop on a story, he has actually gotten a beat if he obtained the information by honorable means (Follett, 1966). Similarly, a *workaholic* should be a *workic*, because the suffix *-ic* in *alcoholic* denotes the addiction; if *workaholic* is correct, then *alcoholaholic* must also be correct. These expressions are all "incorrect," but if we speak of helical staircases, reporters beating a story, or workics, we will not be communicating effectively. People won't know what we mean, and that is what is important.

An analogous situation from procedure writing would occur when someone complained that a step that says, *Open the valve*, is incorrect because the user isn't opening a valve, he's flipping a switch. The distinction is meaningless—assuming that users are trained to know which switch operates the valve.

Similar problems can occur with conditional steps. Consider the following: *IF, at <u>any</u> time while performing this procedure, an operating diesel generator's 4.16 kv bus is de-energized, <u>THEN</u> energize the 4.16 kv vital bus*. A complaint with this step might be that there are actually two conditions in the antecedent: a diesel generator must be operating and its 4.16 kv bus must be de-energized. Thus, a more "correct" way to write the step would be, *<u>IF</u>, at <u>any</u> time while performing this procedure, a diesel generator is operating <u>AND</u> its 4.16 kv bus in de-energized, <u>THEN</u> energize the vital 4.16 kv bus*. But this version may be more difficult to understand. Because this step is taken from a procedure that addresses a loss of off-site power, it is a reasonable assumption that a diesel generator will be running, so the first condition will always be met. The second condition is the critical condition, but, by appearing as the second of two conditions, it is not emphasized as heavily. An alternative might be to recast the step, maintaining the two conditions: _IF, at any time while performing this procedure, a 14.6 kv bus is de-energized AND that bus is linked to an operating diesel generator, THEN energize the 4.16 kv vital bus._ But this alternative is longer and worded more awkwardly. Both of these alternatives are solutions to a non-existent problem—the initial wording of the step was clear and concise.

True, this is a complex and subtle point, but, as a procedure writer, you will be dealing with issues such as these on a daily basis. Obviously, the rules governing conditional terms are important and must be followed; 95 percent of the time they will lead to steps that are clear and easy to understand. But you have some leeway in how you apply these rules, and this is an instance where a rigid interpretation of rules governing conditional terms—in pursuit of a step that is more "correct"—in actuality makes the step more difficult to understand. This example also illustrates the point made in Section 21.1, that you cannot cookbook the procedure writing process. The rules on conditional terms have to be applied with an eye towards the writer's craft.

This discussion is not intended to dismiss the importance of correct procedures, of course. The intention is to convey the point that a procedure is correct if its users will understand it in the manner the writer intended. It is as simple as that. Debates over the "correctness" of a word or step are rendered moot if users will interpret the word or step in the manner intended. That's the final standard.

21.3 Consistency

One theme that occurs over and over again in this book is that of consistency. We're returning to it once more because consistency is important—it's the hallmark of a good procedure. Similar thoughts should be expressed in a similar manner, or else the writer runs the risk that the reader will perceive his writing as undisciplined or, worse, will attribute differences in meaning to spurious differences in presentation. Take the time yourself to review procedures for consistency and then get someone else to look at them. It is that important.

21.4   Don't Blame Everything on the Procedure

One of the authors of this book was witnessing an exercise in a nuclear power plant where an operator misread a step. This step contained a list of actions that the operator misinterpreted as a list of conditions. As a result, he made an error. In the briefing following the exercise, the problem was discussed and one observer suggested that the action verb be underlined so that it would be clear that the step was, in fact, an action.

Other people involved in the briefing hesitated to agree with this change. The step was clearly written and did not include conditional terms, so there was no clue as to what had confused the user. They wondered why the operator had misread the verb. Would underlining help?

Their concerns were well founded. What had actually happened was that the operator simply wasn't paying attention to the procedure. That happens. And, if the user isn't paying *any* attention to the procedure, it can be the most usable procedure in the world and it will not improve task performance. So underlining the action verb would not have made any difference and would have made the procedure more difficult for a user who was paying attention to understand. He would wonder why that action verb and no other action verb was underlined. Was it somehow different? Thus, emphasizing the action in response to this situation would have been the wrong thing to do.

This example demonstrates several things. First, emphasis is not the answer to every problem. Second, changes to procedures should not be made based on one incident if that incident was a fluke. Finally, don't always blame the procedure when something goes wrong.

This last point is important. True, many errors can be attributed to procedures; if they could not be, there would be little reason for preparing this book. But too often, the response to *any* human performance problem is to revise the procedure or write a new one. Some problems are the result of inexperience, inattention, a lack of training, or even deliberate malice. These problems have nothing to do with procedures. If a procedure is changed to "address" these problems, the result is frequently that the true cause of the problem has not been addressed and the procedure is more difficult to use. Fixing individual bits of procedures due to individual errors can introduce tremendous inconsistencies into procedures. Over-proceduralization, where there is a procedure for everything, can also result. In this situation, users may be more likely to resent procedures because they are words and difficult to use; this resentment can lead to errors in those instances where a procedure is necessary, but the user fails to use the procedure or pays only cursory attention to it.

21.5   Writer Knowledge Versus User Knowledge

For the most part in procedure writing, it is appropriate for procedure writers to view their users as people who know less than the writers about the *specific information* covered in the procedures. This is not to say that the readers know less about the system, process, or equipment covered in the procedure than the writer, nor is it to say that the writer is necessarily smarter or wiser than the reader. However, the writer generally has access to many resources that are unavailable to the procedure user. For example, when attempting to determine the best way to perform some task, the writer may consult numerous basis documents; interview technical experts; interview users; draft different versions of the procedure and test them in simulations; and, perhaps most importantly, take time to think about, ponder, and mull over the options. Procedure users rarely have such luxuries. The user must decide upon a course of action and take it. This difference, in fact, is one of the basic reasons for writing procedures at all—in order to allow someone to take the time to find the best way of performing a task and documenting that method to help others perform the task.

This premise that the writer knows more (or at least had access to more resources) than the reader is reflected in numerous aspects of the form and use of procedures. Perhaps most importantly, this premise is reflected in the content of procedures. For example, as explained in the discussion of equally acceptable steps, the writer should not tell the reader about every method by which a task could be performed, the writer should (usually) choose the best method and present that method only in the procedure. However, the discussion of equally acceptable steps also stated that sometimes the writer should provide the reader with options. Why should the writer let the reader select from among options when, presumably, the writer has more resources than the reader for making such decisions? Quite simply, despite all of the advantages the writer has over the reader for acquiring and analyzing information, he or she does not always know more than the reader does about the specific information presented in the procedure, because the reader knows (or at least has the opportunity to know) things about the equipment, process, or system covered in the procedure that are unique to the particular moment that the procedure is being executed. The fact that the reader has access to such information, which the writer cannot possibly obtain, underlies the general principle presented here.

The general principle, then, is that the writer should provide the reader with options only when the reader has information that informs decisions (or judgments) that the writer cannot obtain. Generally this information is limited to the status of the system or equipment documented in the procedure that will vary from one occasion to another. When such variables affect the optimum way that the procedure should be performed, the writer should not only allow the user to make decisions or judgments but should either force the user to do so (e.g., through conditional statements that demand that the user assess the status of the system and make decisions based upon the outcome of those decisions) or encourage the user to do so (e.g., through equally acceptable steps or unconditional external cross-references). If possible, the writer should simplify the decision making for the user by giving the user objective decision criteria upon which to base decisions. Regardless of how variable the system is, the writer still has the luxury of time to assess alternatives. Thus, the writer can figure out exactly what options might be available and what factors favor each option. On some occasions, however, the variables become too numerous and too far-reaching for the writer to simplify the decision-making process by incorporating decision points for all of the variables into the procedure. It is at this point that the writer should turn the responsibility of choosing approaches over to the user and let the user make judgments. Once the writer has made this decision, his responsibilities expand to making sure that the reader is told what he or she needs to know to make informed judgments (e.g., global and contextual information about the procedure become more important than ever).

In summary, writers should attempt to find the best way of performing tasks and document those methods in procedures. When this is not possible, writers should attempt to provide users with objective criteria for making decisions (e.g., conditional statements). The least preferred presentation, but a correct choice on some occasions, is to simply provide users with options and the information needed to make informed judgments. The choice of presentation will depend upon the relative amounts of information available to the writer and the user. As the amount of relevant information that is available to the user but not the writer increases, so should the amount of choice handed over to the user.

As a final note, the principle discussed here might be broadened just a bit further to state the single principle that underlies all of the guidance presented here. This principle might also be considered the single fundamental core principle of effective procedure writing. This global principle, simply stated, is "honor thy user."

Glossary

acronyms: Acronyms are abbreviations for a group of words, formed from the first letter of each word. Periods do not separate letters in an acronym. Often, acronyms themselves are pronounced like words. For example, the acronym NASA (pronounced *nah-suh*) stands for the National Aeronautics and Space Administration.

action verb: An action verb is a verb that directs the user to perform a task in an action step. The action verb is typically the first word in the step.

action step: See step.

active voice: Active voice is a sentence construction that shows the subject of the sentence acting. For example, *John checked out the book* is an active voice sentence. In a passive voice sentence, the subject is being acted upon, as in *The book was checked out by John.*

appendix: Supplementary material at the end of the procedure. Appendices include information that covers a specific subject or function. They are required for procedure completion but are used separately. An example of an appendix is a checklist. Appendices are sometimes called attachments.

attachment: See appendix.

blocks of text: Blocks of text are groups of words.

bold type: Bold type is heavier and darker than regular type. Bold type contrasts more with its white background and captures the reader's attention more quickly, provided that it (or other emphasis techniques) are not overused.

case: The case of a noun changes depending on whether the noun form is subjective (we), objective (us), or possessive (our). Case also refers to capital letters (upper case) and smaller letters (lower case). See type case.

cautions: Cautions alert users to potential hazards in conditions, practices, or procedures that may damage products and equipment or adversely affect site operations. See warnings.

check-off spaces: A box or line on which to place a checkmark to indicate that a step has been successfully completed.

coding techniques: Coding techniques are emphasis techniques that identify information; for example, full capitalization and underlining identifies conditional terms.

concurrent steps: Concurrent steps are two or more steps that are performed at the same time.

conditional cross-reference: A cross-reference in a conditional statement:

> IF the steam generator levels can maintain heat removal,
> THEN GO TO Step [5] in this procedure.

conditional statements: Also called logic statements, conditional statements are instructions that indicate an action should be performed only if certain conditions are met. Conditional terms such as IF, WHEN, THEN, NOT, AND and OR are used to present conditional statements.

conditional terms: IF, WHEN, THEN, NOT, IF NOT, AND, and OR. Conditional terms are used in conditional statements according to the rules of Boolean logic.

continuous steps: Continuous steps are those that apply for a period of time while the procedure is being executed.

cover page: The cover page is the first page of the procedure.

cross-references: A cross-reference is a reference from one section of a procedure to another part of the same procedure or to a different procedure.

diagnostic steps: Steps that assist users in determining the nature of a situation. A flowchart is often a useful format for diagnostic steps.

emphasis techniques: Emphasis techniques are the typographical, spatial, or graphic techniques that emphasize or code information in the procedure.

equally acceptable steps: These are steps that specify a number of equally acceptable alternative actions.

font: A font is all the characters and punctuation marks of one style of type.

format: The way the pages of a document look.

framing: Enclosing in a box.

grammar: The written official rules, and unwritten common-knowledge rules, governing how words are put together to form a language. Grammar concerns spoken as well as written communication.

headings: Headings are short phrases that introduce the beginning of a section by describing that section.

Helvetica: Helvetica is a common sans serif typeface. This sentence is written in Helvetica.

hierarchy: A hierarchy is a group of ideas organized or classified according to rank or importance.

human factors: Human factors is the discipline that studies how human beings interact with technology as well as how technology affects human performance, primarily in industrial settings.

imperative mode: A sentence in the imperative mode (or mood) is considered a command. It is understood that the subject of the sentence is *you* although this word is not used. The sentence *Check the SI system in one hour* is written in the imperative mode.

ITC Avant Garde Gothic Book: A sans serif typeface. This sentence is written in ITC Avant Garde Gothic Book.

justified text: Text with straight margins on the left and right, so that every line begins and ends the same distance from the left or right margin.

left-justified text: Text that is aligned along the left margin of a page.

level of detail: The amount of technical detail presented in a procedure. Steps that are written at a low level of detail include only general instructions and rely heavily on user training. Steps that are written at a high level of detail precisely specify all actions.

line spacing: Line spacing is the dimension measured perpendicularly from the baseline of one line of text to the baseline of the next line.

logic statements: See conditional statements.

logic terms: See conditional terms.

margins: A uniform amount of white space at the top, bottom, right side, and left side of a page.

model: A representation of a process. For example, a model of the reading process helps people understand how people gain information from printed text.

New Century Schoolbook: A serif typeface. This sentence is written in New Century Schoolbook.

nonsequential steps: These are steps that appear where they are first required but that may need to be performed later in the sequence of actions. Nonsequential steps include continuous steps, time-dependent steps, and repeated steps.

notes: Notes provide important supplemental non-safety-related information to users. Information may be presented in a note if it would otherwise be difficult to incorporate into the procedure.

objective, statement of: A brief description of the purpose of a procedure that appears at the beginning of the procedure.

Palatino: A serif typeface. This sentence is written in Palatino.

passive voice: Passive voice is a sentence construction in which the subject of the sentence is acted upon. Passive voice sentences always use some form of *to be* in front of the verb. They have the potential to become wordy or confusing; therefore, active voice is usually preferable to passive voice. *The pump was activated by the operator* is an example of a passive voice sentence. See active voice.

placekeeping aids: Placekeeping aids are used to help the user know what steps have been accomplished in a procedure. Check-off boxes are one type of placekeeping aid used to indicate that an action has been accomplished.

point: A typographical measure equal to 1/72 inch.

positive statement: A sentence that does not contain a negative form of a verb is a positive statement. For example, *Do not leave the door open* is a negative statement. *Leave the door closed* is a positive statement that has the same meaning as the negative statement. Positive statements are generally easier to understand.

punctuation: The set of standard symbols used in writing to separate words into sentences, phrases, and clauses, and to help a reader understand the text.

ragged-right margins: When the white space along the right side of a page varies according to line lengths of text, the right margin is ragged (i.e., uneven).

range: An amount of acceptable variation in an instrument reading.

readability: The ease with which a person can read and understand text.

recurrent steps: Recurrent are steps that are performed repeatedly at various times.

repeated steps: See recurrent steps.

right-justified text: Text that is aligned along the right margin of a page.

sans serif: Literally, *without serifs*. Sans serif fonts do not have short lines at the end of the strokes in their letters.

schema: A schema is a mental structure that represents a person's knowledge of the world based on personal experience. People constantly build new schemata (the plural of *schema*) and add to old schemata as they encounter experiences each day. These schemata help people interpret and store information gained through these experiences. For example, while reading text a person might draw from a schema for punctuation marks that helps the person know that periods signify the end of a sentence.

serif: The short lines at the end of the strokes in letters in some typefaces are called serifs.

single-column format: A format where the text forms one column.

spacing, line: See line spacing.

spatial emphasis: Use of white space to highlight information.

step: A step provides instructions for performing a specific action.

symbols: Symbols are printed or written signs used to represent an operation, element, quantity, quality, or relation.

syntax: Syntax is the way in which words are combined to form phrases and sentences.

time-dependent steps: Steps that are performed after a set period of time has passed. When presenting a time-dependent step, it is important to provide space for users to note the time that "starts the clock" and to present a calculation aid that will enable them to calculate the time at which the action should be taken.

Times: Also called Times Roman, this serif typeface is commonly used for large blocks of text because it is considered very readable. This book is written in Times.

transitions: See cross-references.

true emphasis techniques: Emphasis techniques that identify important information. See coding techniques.

twelve-point type: This is a type font's specified size based on characters of the font formerly having been cast in lead blocks that measured 12 points high. Different fonts that are all twelve-point type fonts will look different in size because the widths and heights of individual characters in each font vary from one another.

two-column format: Procedures that are presented in two columns. The left-hand column can present actions while the right-hand column presents details. An alternative two-column format presents the actions in the left-hand column and contingencies in the right-hand column.

type case: Type case refers to whether letters are presented in all capitals, mixed case, or all lower case. For blocks of text, mixed case is easier to read than all capitals.

type face: See font.

type size: This dimension pertains to the height of a block of lead in which a letter would have been cast. Type size is typically greater than the actual height of letters in a typeface.

typography: Typography is the arrangement and appearance of type on a page.

validation: A formal check of a procedure's accuracy and usability. Technically, verification and validation are two separate processes, although they are often considered as one. Comprehensive verification and validation consists of simulator exercises, control room and plant walkthroughs, and desktop reviews.

verification: See validation.

visual angle: Visual angle is the angle subtended at the eye by a letter of type (or anything else on the page). When determining the optimal type size for a printed document, writers can use a formula to calculate the visual angle and to ensure that typed characters are sufficiently large for the viewer's eye to discern at a given distance.

walkdown: A walkdown consists of physically visiting and observing the location in which the activities are to be performed and the equipment that will be used. A walkdown is performed to ensure that the equipment and environment are actually as envisioned and the people involved can perform the required tasks.

walkthrough: A walkthrough is the cumulative, detailed check of a process and facility. Activities that may be used to complete walkthroughs include walkdowns, simulations, or modeling.

warnings: Warnings alert procedure users to potential hazards that may lead to death, injury, or radioactive release. See cautions.

white space: White space is blank space on a printed page. White space commonly defines the margins of a page and separates lines of text, words, and characters from one another on a printed page.

x-height: The height of the lower-case letter x (and a, c, e, and so on) in a font of type. If graphic designers use the visual angle formula to determine the optimal type size for a document, they should equate the results of that formula with the x-height of the letters in a font rather than with the font size itself.

References

American Nuclear Society. (1989). *American National Standard Administrative Controls and Quality Assurance for the Operational Phase of Nuclear Power Plants* (ANSI/ANS-3.2-1988). La Grange Park, IL: Author.

Anderson, B. (1963). "The short-term retention of active and passive sentences." Unpublished doctoral dissertation, Johns Hopkins University. Cited in Coleman, 1963.

Anderson, P.V. (1991). *Technical Writing: A Reader-Oriented Approach* (2nd Ed.). San Diego, CA: Harcourt Brace Jovanovich.

Anderson, R.C., Reynolds, R.E., Schallert, D.L., & Goetz, E.T. (1977). Frameworks for comprehending discourse. *American Educational Research Journal, 14*(4), 367-381.

Bailey, R.W. (1982). *Human Performance Engineering: A Guide For System Designers.* Engelwood Cliffs, NJ: Prentice-Hall, Inc.

Ballard, J.C., & Rode-Perkins, S.L. (1987). How to create mass media print warnings. *Technical Communication, 34*(2), 84-88.

Barfield, W. (1986). Expert-novice differences for software: Implications for problem-solving and knowledge acquisition. *Behavior and Information Technology, 5*, 15-29.

Barnes, V.E., Bramwell, A.T., Olson, J., Wieringa, D.R., & Wilson, R.A. (in press). *The Extent, Nature, Causes, and Consequences of Procedure Violations in U.S. Nuclear Power Plants: A Follow-up to Chernobyl* (NUREG/CR-5786). Washington, DC: Nuclear Regulatory Commission.

Barnes, V.E., Moore, C.J., Wieringa, D.R., Isakson, C.S., Kono, B.K., & Gruel, R.L. (1989). *Techniques for Preparing Flowchart-Format Emergency Operating Procedures* (NUREG/CR-5228). Washington, DC: Nuclear Regulatory Commission.

Barnes, V.E., & Radford, L.R. (1987). *Evaluation of Nuclear Power Plant Operating Procedures Classifications and Interfaces* (NUREG/CR-4613). Washington, DC: Nuclear Regulatory Commission.

Benson, P.J. (1985). Writing visually: Design considerations in technical publications. *Technical Communication, 32*(4). 35-39.

Berkin, M.M. (1964). Performance decrement under psychological stress. *Human Factors, 6,* 21-30.

Bernstein, T.M. (1965). *The Careful Writer: A Modern Guide to English Usage.* New York: Atheneum.

Berry, E. (1981). How to get users to follow procedures. *Journal of Systems Management, 1,* 22-25.

Bovair, S., & Kieras, D.E. (1989). *Toward a Model of Acquiring Procedures from Text* (Report No. 30). Ann Arbor, MI: University of Michigan.

Brooke, J., & Duncan, K. (1981). Effects of system display format on performance in a fault location task. *Ergonomics, 24,* 175-189.

Brusaw, C.T., Alred, G.J., & Oliu, W.E. (1987). *Handbook of Technical Writing.* New York: St. Martin's Press.

Burnett, R.E. (1990). *Technical Communication* (Second Edition). Belmont, CA: Wadsworth.

Chall, J.S. (1984). Readability and prose comprehension: Continuities and discontinuities. *Understanding Reading Comprehension: Cognition, Language, and the Structure of Prose* (pp. 233-247). Newark, DE: International Reading Association.

The Chicago Manual of Style: For Authors, Editors, and Copywriters (13th Ed.). (1982). Chicago, IL: University of Chicago Press.

Coleman, E.B. (1963). Learning of prose written in four grammatical transformations. *Journal of Applied Psychology, 47*(5), 332-341.

Dixon, P. (1987). Actions and procedural directions. *Coherence and Grounding in Discourse* (pp. 70-89). Philadelphia, PA: John Benjamins Publishing Co.

Duchastel, P.C. (1982). Textural display techniques. In D.H. Jonassen (Ed.), *The Technology of Text* (pp. 167-192). Englewood Cliffs, NJ: Educational Technology Publications.

Duffy, T.M. (1985). Preparing technical manuals: Specifications and guidelines. In D.H. Jonassen (Ed.), *The Technology of Text: Volume Two* (pp. 370-392). Englewood Cliffs, NJ: Educational Technology Publications.

Dye, K.L. (1988). When is a document accurate and complete? *IPCC 1988 Conference Record: On the Edge: A Pacific Rim Conference on Technical Communication,* Seattle, Washington, October 5-7, 1988 (pp. 269-272). New York: Institute of Electrical and Electronic Engineers.

Echeverria, D., Barnes, V., Bittner, A., Fawcett-Long, J., Moore, C., Terrill, B., Westra, C., Wieringa, D., & Wilson, R. (in press). *The Impact of Environmental Exposures on Human Performance: Volumes I and II* (NUREG/CR-5680 and NUREG/CR-7675). Washington, DC: Nuclear Regulatory Commission.

Farkas, D., & Farkas, N. (1981). Manuscript surprises: A problem in copy editing. *Technical Communication, 28*(2), 12-22.

Follett, W. (1966). *Modern American Usage: A Guide.* New York: Hill and Wang.

Fuchs, F., Engelschall, J., & Imlay, G. (1981). *Human Engineering Guidelines for Use in Preparing Emergency Operating Procedures for Nuclear Power Plants* (NUREG/CR-1999). Washington, DC: Nuclear Regulatory Commission.

Giles, T.D. (1990). The readability controversy: A technical writing review. *Journal of Technical Writing and Communication, 20*(2), 131-138.

Glynn, S.M., Britton, B.K., & Tillman, M.H. (1985). Typographical cues in text: Management of the reader's attention. In D.H. Jonassen (Ed.), *The Technology of Text: Volume Two* (pp. 192-209). Englewood Cliffs, NJ: Educational Technology Publications.

Green, T.R. (1977). Conditional program statements and comprehensibility to professional programmers. *Journal of Occupational Psychology, 50*, 93-109.

Gringas, B. (1987). Simplified English in maintenance manuals. *Technical Communication, 34*(1), 24-28.

Harbaugh, F.W. (1991). Accentuate the positive. *Technical Communication, 38*(1), 73-74.

Harris, J.E., & Wiklund, M.E. (1989). Consumer acceptance of threatening warnings in the residential environment. *Proceedings of the Human Factors Society 33rd Annual Meeting* (pp. 989-993). Santa Monica, CA: Human Factors Society.

Hartley, J. (1982). Designing instructional text. In D.H. Jonassen (Ed.), *The Technology of Text* (pp. 193-214). Englewood Cliffs, NJ: Educational Technology Publications.

Hartley, J. (1985). *Designing Instructional Text* (2nd Ed.). New York: Nichols.

Hartley, J., & Burnhill, P. (1977). Fifty guidelines for improving instructional text. *Programmed Learning and Educational Technology, 14*(1), 65-75.

Hartley, J., & Jonassen, D.H. (1985). The role of headings in printed and electronic text. In D.H. Jonassen (Ed.), *The Technology of Text: Volume Two* (pp. 237-263). Englewood Cliffs, NJ: Educational Technology Publications.

Hartley, J., & Trueman, M. (1983). The effects of headings in text on recall, search and retrieval. *British Journal of Educational Psychology, 53*, 205-214.

Herriot, P. (1969). Comprehension of active and passive sentences as a function of pragmatic expectations. *Journal of Verbal Learning and Verbal Behavior, 8,* 166-169.

Holland, V., Charrow, V., & Wright, W. (1988). How can technical writers write effectively for several audiences at once? In L. Beene & P. White (Eds.), *Solving Problems in Technical Writing* (pp. 27-54). New York: Oxford University Press.

Horn, R.E., & Kelly, J.N. (1981). *Structured Writing: An Approach to the Documentation of Computer Software.* Waltham, MA: Information Mapping, Inc.

Houp, K.W., & Pearsall, T.E. (1988). *Reporting Technical Information* (6th Ed.). New York: Collier Macmillan.

Huckin, T.N. (1983). A cognitive approach to readability. In P.V. Anderson, R.J. Brockmann, & C.R. Miller (Eds.), *New Essays in Technical and Scientific Communication: Research, Theory, Practice* (pp. 90-110). New York: Baywood Publishing Company.

Internal Revenue Service. (1990). *Form 1040.* Washington, DC: Author.

James, G. (1985). *Document Databases.* New York: Van Nostrand Reinhold.

Jeffrey, R.C. (1967). *Formal Logic: Its Scope and Limits.* New York: McGraw-Hill.

Jonassen, D.H. (1982). Introduction to section one: Implicit structures in text. In D.H. Jonassen (Ed.), *The Technology of Text* (pp. 5-14). Englewood Cliffs, NJ: Educational Technology Publications.

Kammann, R. (1975). The comprehensibility of printed instructions and the flowchart alternative. *Human Factors, 17*(2), 183-191.

Kantowitz, B.H., & Sorkin, R.D. (1983). *Human Factors: Understanding People-System Relationships.* New York: John Wiley and Sons.

Kieras, D.E. (1978). Good and bad structure in simple paragraphs: Effects on apparent theme, reading time, and recall. *Journal of Verbal Learning and Verbal Behavior, 17,* 13-28.

Lannon, J.M. (1991). *Technical Writing* (5th Ed.). New York: Harper Collins.

Larkin, J.H., & Simon, H.A. (1987). Why a diagram is (sometimes) worth ten thousand words. *Cognitive Science, 11,* 65-99.

Lorch, R.F. Jr., & Lorch, E.P. (1985). Topic structure representation and text recall. *Journal of Educational Psychology, 77*(2), 137-148.

Mackh, G.E., & Rew, L.J. (1991). Using access aids to boost information retrieval. *Technical Communication, 38*(2), 210-219.

Marshall, S.L. (1978). *Men Against Fire: The Problem of Battle Command in Future War.* Glouchester, MA: Peter Smith.

McCarthy, R.L., Finnegan, J.P., Krumm-Scott, S., & McCarthy, G.E. (1984). Product information presentation, user behavior, and safety. *Proceedings of the Human Factors Society 28th Annual Meeting.* Palo Alto, CA: Human Factors Society.

Meyer, B.J. (1985). Signaling the structure of text. In D.H. Jonassen (Ed.), *The Technology of Text: Volume Two* (pp. 64-89). Englewood Cliffs, NJ: Educational Technology Publications.

Moore, C.J., Kono, B.K., Wieringa, D.R., Barnes, V.E., Isakson, C.S., & Gruel, R.L. (1990). "Graphic design tools for promoting the usability of flowchart-format procedures and other functional graphic images." Proceedings of the Society for Technical Communication 3rd Region 7 Conference, Portland, OR., October 12-13, 1990 (pp. 94-107). Arlington, VA: Society for Technical Communication.

Morgenstern, M.H., Barnes, V.E., Radford, L.R., Wheeler, W.A., & Badalamente, R.V. (1985). *Development, Use and Control of Maintenance Procedures in Nuclear Power Plants: Problems and Recommendations* (NUREG/CR-3817). Washington, DC: Nuclear Regulatory Commission.

Nuclear Regulatory Commission (NRC). (1982). *Guidelines for the Preparation of Emergency Operating Procedures* (NUREG-0899). Washington, DC: Author.

Parker, R.C. (1988). *Looking Good in Print: A Guide to Basic Design for Desktop Publishing.* Chapel Hill, NC: Ventana Press.

Payne, J.W. (1976). Task complexity and contingent processing in decision making: An information search and protocol analysis. *Organizational Behavior and Human Performance, 16*(2), 366-387.

Porter, K. (1991). Usage of the passive voice. *Technical Communication, 38*(1), 87-88.

Poulton, B. & Brown, C.H. (1968). Rate of comprehension of an existing teleprinter output and of possible alternatives. *Journal of Applied Psychology, 52,* 16-21.

Poulton, E.C. (1972). Size, style, and vertical spacing in the legibility of small typefaces. *Journal of Applied Psychology, 56,* 156-161.

The Random House Dictionary of the English Language. (1967). New York: Random House.

Rogers, W.H., & Moeller, G. (1984). Comparison of abbreviation methods: Measures of preference and decoding performance. *Human Factors, 26*(1), 49-59.

Shaw, H. (1963). *Punctuate It Right!* New York: Barnes and Noble.

Sherman, M.A. (1973). Bound to be easier? The negative prefix and sentence comprehension. *Journal of Verbal Learning and Verbal Behavior, 12*, 76-84.

Simon, J. (1980). *Paradigms Lost: Reflections on Literacy and Its Decline.* New York: Clarkson N. Potter.

Slobin, D.I. (1966). Grammatical transformation and sentence comprehension in childhood and adulthood. *Journal of Verbal Learning and Verbal Behavior, 5*, 219-227.

Slovic, P., Fischhoff, B. & Lichtenstein, S. (1982). Facts versus fears: Understanding perceived risk. In D. Kahneman, P. Slovic, & A. Tversky (Eds.), *Judgment Under Uncertainty: Heuristics and Biases.* Cambridge, MA: Cambridge University Press.

Smith, S.L. (1979). Letter size and legibility. *Human Factors, 21*(6), 661-670.

Souther, J.W., & White, M.L. (1984). *Technical Report Writing.* Malabar, FL: Robert E. Kriegger Publishing Company.

Spyridakis, J.H. (1989a). Signaling effects: A review of the research—Part I. *Journal of Technical Writing and Communication, 19*(3), 227-240.

Spyridakis, J.H. (1989b). Signaling effects: Increased content retention and new answers—Part II. *Journal of Technical Writing and Communication, 19*(4), 395-421.

Spyridakis, J.H., & Standal, T.C. (1987). Signals in expository prose: Effects on reading comprehension. *Reading Research Quarterly, 22*(3), 285-298.

Spyridakis, J.H., & Wenger, M.J. (1990). Cognitive dimensions of reading comprehension. *Proceedings of the Society for Technical Communication* (3rd Region 7 Conference, Portland, OR., October 12-13 1990) (pp. 124-128). Arlington, VA: Society for Technical Communication.

Stevens, K.C. (1981). Chunking material as an aid to reading comprehension. *Journal of Reading, 25*(2), 126-129.

Sticht, T. (1985). Understanding readers and their uses of texts. In T.M. Duffy & R. Waller (Eds.), *Designing Usable Texts* (pp. 315-340). New York: Academic Press.

Stratton, C.R. (1984). *Technical Writing: Process and Product.* New York: Holt, Rinehart and Winston.

Strunk, W. & White, E.B. (1979). *The Elements of Style* (3rd Ed.). New York: Macmillan.

Tinker, M.A. (1955). Prolonged reading tasks in visual research. *Journal of Applied Psychology, 39*, 444-446.

Tinker, M.A., & Paterson, D.G. (1928). Influence of type form on speed reading. *Journal of Applied Psychology, 12,* 359-368.

Towell, J. (Ed.). (1989). *Acronyms, Initialisms, and Abbreviations Dictionary* (13th Ed., Vol. 1). Detroit, MI: Gale Research Inc.

Trollip, S.R., & Sales, G. (1986). Readability of computer-generated fill-justified text. *Human Factors, 28*(2), 159-163.

Turnbull, A.T., & Baird, R.N. (1980). *The Graphics of Communication* (4th Ed.). New York: Holt, Rinehart, and Winston.

Tversky, A. & Kahneman, D. (1982). Judgment under uncertainty: Heuristics and biases. In D. Kahneman, P. Slovic, & A. Tversky (Eds.), *Judgment Under Uncertainty: Heuristics and Biases* (pp. 2-20). Cambridge, MA: Cambridge University Press.

Vartabedian, A.G. (1971). The effects of letter size, case, and generation method on CRT display search time. *Human Factors, 13,* 363-368.

Waller, R. (1982). Text as diagram: Using typography to improve access and understanding. In D.H. Jonassen (Ed.), *The Technology of Text* (pp. 137-166). Englewood Cliffs, NJ: Educational Technology Publications.

Washington State Office of Financial Management. (1990). *Investment in Human Capital Study: Executive Summary and Synthesis.* Olympia, WA: Author.

Wason, P.C. (1959). The processing of positive and negative information. *Quarterly Journal of Experimental Psychology, 11,* 92-107.

Wason, P.C. (1961). Responses to affirmative and negative binary statements. *British Journal of Psychology, 52,* 133-142.

Wason, P.C. (1968). The drafting of rules. *The New Law Journal, 118*(5341), 548-549.

Webster's New Collegiate Dictionary. (1977). Springfield, MA: Merriam.

Weiss, E.H. (1990). Visualizing a procedure with Nassi-Schneiderman charts. *Journal of Technical Writing and Communication, 20*(3), 237-254.

Wogalter, M.S., Godfrey, S.A., & Fontenelle, G.A. (1987). Effectiveness of warnings. *Human Factors, 29*(5), 599-612.

Words Into Type. (1974). Englewood Cliffs, NJ: Prentice-Hall, Inc.

Wright, P. (1985). Is evaluation a myth? Assessing text assessment procedures. In D.H. Jonassen (Ed.), *The Technology of Text: Volume Two* (pp. 418-436). Englewood Cliffs, NJ: Educational Technology Publications.

Wright, P., & Reid, F. (1973). Written information: Some alternatives to prose for expressing the outcomes of complex contingencies. *Journal of Applied Psychology, 57*(2), 160-166.

Zach, S.E. (1980). Control room operating procedures: Content and format. *Proceedings of the Human Factors Society, 24th Annual Meeting* (pp. 125-127). Santa Monica, CA: Human Factors Society.

Zimmerman, C.M., & Campbell, J.J. (1988). *Fundamentals of Procedure Writing* (2nd Ed.). Columbia, MD: GP Publishing, Inc.

Index